MORAL RELEVANCE AND
MORAL CONFLICT

MORAL RELEVANCE

AND **MORAL CONFLICT**

James D. Wallace

CORNELL UNIVERSITY PRESS

Ithaca and London

First published 1988 by Cornell University Press.

International Standard Book Number 0-8014-2096-2
Library of Congress Catalog Card Number 87-47961
Printed in the United States of America
Librarians: Library of Congress cataloging information appears on the last page of the book.

The paper in this book is acid-free and meets the guidelines for permanence and durability of the Committee on Production Guidelines for Book Longevity of the Council on Library Resources.

To Frederick L. Will

CONTENTS

PREFACE

IN THE MID-1970s, like many other teachers of philosophy, I succumbed to the pressure to teach courses in "applied" ethics. I soon found that the philosophy I knew did not equip me to deal with my students' reasonable concerns about practical issues, and I decided that this inability was a defect in me as a philosopher. My efforts to remedy that state of affairs led me to change my views about moral philosophy and philosophical methodology. This book about ethical theory and practical reasoning is one result of that change.

My greatest debt in this project is to Frederick L. Will, to whom the book is dedicated. His philosophical work has been a model for me to follow. For both his example and his encouragement I am deeply grateful.

I have benefited considerably from the comments and criticisms of students, colleagues, and others. Marcia Baron, Charles E. Caton, B. J. Diggs, Richard Fern, Lester Hunt, Robert McKim, Amelie Rorty, Roger Sullivan, Steven Wagner, David Foster Wallace, and Gary Watson all helped. I am indebted to them and to others too.

My research was assisted by a grant from the American

Council of Learned Societies under a program funded by the National Endowment for the Humanities and by two grants from the Research Board of the University of Illinois at Urbana-Champaign. The generous support of these agencies is acknowledged with thanks.

Linda Conway has prepared several successive typescripts of this work with great care and efficiency. John G. Ackerman of Cornell University Press has been helpful and encouraging at every stage of the project. Sally Foster Wallace, my wife, has helped in matters of writing style and has offered loving support in good times and bad. I have been very fortunate.

JAMES D. WALLACE

Urbana, Illinois

MORAL RELEVANCE AND
MORAL CONFLICT

INTRODUCTION

WE ARE OFTEN confronted with the following sort of practical problem. A moral consideration — one that makes a difference to us — clearly indicates a certain course of action, while an altogether different moral consideration, which also has a strong claim upon us, indicates a contrary course of action. This is a conflict problem. Another sort of practical problem arises when there is a moral consideration that, *if* it were relevant to the problem at hand, would clearly indicate a certain sort of action, but it is unclear whether the consideration is relevant, and we are uncertain. This is a relevance problem. Relevance and conflict problems are common, and some of them are very difficult.

An acceptable moral philosophy should be able to explain how moral relevance and conflict problems are properly resolved, but the most commonly held moral theories do not provide satisfactory accounts of these matters. This book begins with an explanation and defense of these claims. Chapter 2 offers a diagnosis of the sources of the difficulties with the standard accounts of these matters. The succeeding chapters expound, defend, and illustrate an account of how relevance and conflict

[1]

problems are properly resolved which is intended to be free of the difficulties of the standard accounts.

The standard accounts of how moral relevance and conflict problems are properly resolved are rivals, but they share certain deep assumptions about morality and practical reasoning. Among these is the assumption that there exist fixed, unchanging rules or methods that provide explicit directions for the solution of such problems. In order to produce an account of these matters that is free from the difficulties of the standard accounts, one must give up such assumptions, but this has far-reaching consequences. The account I offer of how relevance and conflict problems are properly resolved is based upon a particular conception of morality and practical reasoning. The view is not original, but it is unfamiliar to many contemporary students of moral philosophy. It rejects some of the central assumptions that underlie current discussions in the field. The subject matter of philosophical ethics may look strange and unfamiliar at first from the perspective I advocate: the view is neither deontological nor consequentialist; it is neither an act-theory nor a rule-theory. The view rejects the assumptions upon which these distinctions are based. On this view, the contrast between moral and nonmoral practical considerations is not always a sharp one, and morality itself is something that moves and changes.

Most moral philosophers disagree with these claims, but a strong case can be made for such a view. In its barest outline, the argument is this. The assumptions upon which the standard views are based make it impossible to understand how moral relevance and conflict problems can be resolved by rational means. If, however, such problems cannot be resolved by such means, the claim that morality offers resources by which intelligent people should guide their lives becomes implausible. If one wants to hold that morality provides such a guide, these assumptions must be given up and an alternative sought. The view I advocate is pragmatic (in the philosophical sense)

[2]

and contextualist. Reasons for adopting it include its fit with the denial of the problematic assumptions of the standard views and its ability to explain how relevance and conflict problems are properly resolved. The aim of this book is to present these reasons as cogently as possible. It may be of use to the reader to have at the outset a brief description of my view of practical reasoning and ethics.

Positive morality is seen here as a body of practical knowledge. It has its uses — many different uses; much of the basis for criticizing morality, re-forming morality, and appreciating it comes from the degree of its aptness for these uses. There are important differences between the sort of practical knowledge embodied in morality and technical practical knowledge of the sort employed by those who build and repair clocks (or design internal combustion engines, compose music, test drugs for medical effectiveness, and so on). There are, however, important similarities that are neglected to the detriment of moral philosophy.

Practical knowledge is gleaned from the experience of individuals and groups of individuals in dealing with concrete practical problems. People share their knowledge, and it is transmitted to others who may thereby benefit from the discoveries of someone else and perhaps contribute from their own ingenuity and experience. The development of technical practical knowledge does not affect the practice of technicians alone. In some cases, such developments affect profoundly the way everyone lives — the invention of the clock provides an interesting example.[1] Such developments stimulate new interests and pose unprecedented problems, sometimes in areas of life that seem remote from the activities of technicians. The practical knowledge that is embodied in morality is similarly the product of the experience of individuals with a great many concrete prac-

1. For a history of the measurement of time, see Daniel J. Boorstin, *The Discoverers* (New York: Random House, 1983), Book I.

tical problems. It too is cumulative and changing; it stimulates new concerns and interests and poses new problems that prompt further changes.

On this view it is not surprising that relevance and conflict problems should be so common. A complex, moving world continually poses unprecedented difficulties and novel configurations of difficulties. Our practical knowledge, such as it is, including our morality, is our resource for dealing with such problems, but it was developed in response to a particular set of past problems and circumstances. To bring it to bear upon new problems, we must adapt it, and such adaptation requires intelligence, ingenuity, an understanding of our present circumstances, and a mastery and discriminating understanding of what knowledge we have. In solving unprecedented practical problems, we change our store of practical knowledge, we to a degree alter our aims, standards, and ways. Efforts to solve moral relevance and conflict problems inevitably change morality. Whether such a change is an improvement will depend upon a number of things. First, the particular problem whose solution occasioned the change will have directly confronted us with a certain need. A good solution, of course, will address that need. Our actual concerns, practices, standards, and ideals — the entire body of these things — are complexly interwoven. The adaptation of our practices and standards to deal with a particular problem will have ramifications elsewhere — it may require extensive adjustments in other aims, practices, and the like. The nature and effects of these readjustments will be important considerations in the critical evaluation of the solution to a relevance or conflict problem.

Such a view as this, properly elaborated, can explain how moral relevance and conflict problems are properly resolved; it can provide an account of how we can solve certain important difficult problems by the use of critical intelligence. The view, however, does not offer a decision procedure, an algorithm for solving such problems. In technical practical areas, it is appar-

[4]

ent that there are no algorithms for solving unprecedented problems, and on this view of morality, we should not expect mechanical decision procedures for moral relevance and conflict problems. Such problems are as difficult as circumstances make them. Nothing guarantees that certain of these moral problems will not be so complex and convoluted, so disheartening in the choices they offer us, that we lack sufficient intelligence and courage to solve them. This may be an unwelcome conclusion — one may not like it. If we reflect upon human experience, however, it is not an implausible result.

[1]

Relevance and Conflict Problems

THE RESOLUTION of the more difficult moral problems and the more sharply controverted moral issues often requires us to make determinations about which considerations are relevant, and, when the relevant considerations conflict with one another, to determine what course of action the stronger reasons indicate. In dealing with actual problems, making such determinations can be very hard indeed. Often, this is the problem.

There is very general agreement, for example, that it is morally wrong to hire someone to kill a person to advance one's career, to ease financial burdens, or to relieve oneself of a burdensome dependent. It is a matter of great controversy, however, whether this consideration is relevant to the question of whether it is morally wrong for a pregnant woman to hire someone to destroy the fetus within her to advance her career, and so on. This is an example of what I will call a "relevance problem," and it is a particularly difficult relevance problem. Conflict problems, on the other hand, are engendered by situations in which two or more relevant considerations indicate contrary courses of action. Public officials, for example, have a responsibility to preserve public order and safety. They also should protect individuals who are innocent of any offenses from arrest and judicial punishment. In a time of widespread rioting, looting, and disorder, measures necessary to control disturbances that threaten public order — mass arrests and summary trials, for example — may also substantially increase the possibility that innocent individuals will be arrested and punished. In this situation, to what extent is it justifiable to risk punishing innocent people in order to control riots? How far may public officials risk the public's safety to protect individuals from miscarriages of justice? The answers to these questions will require a determination of the relative importance of these considerations in the particular situation.

Existing theories in moral philosophy are of less help than one would like in solving difficult normative moral problems. One reason for this is that such theories, for various reasons, do not in a useful way address the question of how the determinations necessary to solve relevance and conflict problems properly are made. Most theories, in one way or another, deny the existence of the problem. Classical utilitarians hold that there is but one moral consideration and that this consideration admits of quantitative determination and comparison. Some theorists who follow Kant suppose that since they recognize but one fundamental principle, conflict problems do not arise. Theorists who recognize several moral principles or considerations either suppose that we can simply see (intuit) which consideration takes precedence in particular cases where these conflict, or make it a requirement for a satisfactory set of principles or considerations that these not conflict in actual cases. A number of theoretical devices are used to forestall such conflicts. All these theories are open to serious objections, and actual moral controversy remains embroiled with relevance and conflict problems.

Such at any rate is my contention. Relevance and conflict problems are real — no theoretical conjuring will make them disappear. Further, moral relevance and conflict problems are ubiquitous; their solution is a crucial task of practical reason. If it should turn out that such problems do not admit of solution by rational means, then it is not clear why moral considerations should be of great concern to those committed to seeking intelligent, reasoned solutions to the problems of living. We might choose for sentimental reasons to cherish the ways of our ancestors, like atheists celebrating Christmas, but the body of considerations loosely gathered under the heading of "morality" will fail too often to serve as resources for the intelligent conduct of life.

Western moral philosophy since Plato is substantially concerned with responding to a certain sort of moral skepticism. From our present perspective within this philosophical tradition, the most important things in the ethical theories of Plato, Aristotle, Hume, and Kant are connected with their efforts to show why moral considerations matter at all. For various reasons, we get little help from these philosophers with the questions of what to do in a particular case when the relevance of these considerations is in dispute or where relevant considerations conflict.

The failure of these theories to address these questions in a satisfactory way actually undermines the effectiveness of the theories as refutations of moral skepticism. In the eyes of thoughtful individuals, the difficulty of the intellectual task of determining relevance and harmonizing conflicts of considerations in controversial and complex moral problems lends a certain plausibility to the claim that there are no right solutions to such problems. Unless the skeptical claim that there is no way to determine objectively which solutions are correct is met head on, the suspicion will remain that it is impossible in principle to resolve important moral disagreements by rational means.

I CLAIM that relevance problems are real and very common. Most moral theorists, however, ignore relevance problems and maintain that conflicts among moral considerations are only apparent, that upon a careful scrutiny the conflicts disappear. Very generally, there are two different and incompatible theoretical bases for denying the reality of conflict problems. One type of view holds that although there appear to be many different moral considerations that from time to time conflict with one another, actually this appearance is misleading. There is really but one relevant consideration in any moral problem, according to such views; the many apparently different considerations are somehow reducible to a single consideration. According to classical act-utilitarianism, for example, there is but one valid practical consideration — maximizing utility. Anything else that seems to be a consideration really matters only insofar as it contributes to such maximization. On the second sort of view that denies the reality of conflict problems, many irreducibly different moral considerations exist, but these considerations never really conflict. They only seem to conflict because our conceptions of the considerations are vague, imprecise, or incomplete. Clarity and definiteness also clear up any difficulties about the relevance of these considerations.

It is tempting to suppose that on *any* single-consideration moral theory there cannot be conflict problems and that relevance problems are simplified because one need worry only about the relevance of the single consideration. If, however, one counts as single-consideration views ethical theories that recognize but one (ultimate) principle, not all such views escape serious difficulties with relevance and conflict problems. This will be apparent to anyone who has attempted to apply to a selection of actual moral problems the "supreme principle of morality" as Kant sets it out in the *Grundlegung zur Metaphysik der Sitten*.[1] Kant's principle encounters difficulties with relevance

1. G. E. M. Anscombe pointed out that Kant's principle about universal

and conflict problems not because of some feature unique to it, nor is this a problem only for "formalist" single-principle theories. Consider Ruth Barcan Marcus's example: "Under the single principle of promise keeping, I might make two promises in all good faith and reason that they will not conflict, but they do, as a result of circumstances that were unpredictable and beyond my control."[2]

THUS THE theoretical expediency of recognizing but one ultimate or overriding practical principle will not necessarily exempt us from difficulties with relevance and conflict problems. Classical utilitarianism, however, is a kind of single-

---

izing maxims — one formulation of the supreme principle — is "useless without stipulations as to what shall count as a relevant description of an action with a view to constructing a maxim about it" ("Modern Moral Philosophy," *Philosophy* 33 [1958], 2). Kant is able to argue with some plausibility that if my maxim is to refuse help to a person in desperate need who asks me for help, I cannot will that my maxim hold as a universal law — such a law would rob *me* of help in such circumstances. Suppose I make it my policy (i.e., my maxim) to refuse to help *children*. I, an adult, would not be robbed of help by the currency of a law that permitted refusing to help *children*. Of course, a child is a person, but why for the purposes of describing my maxim is it not *relevant* that the person who asks for my help is *a child*? Answers suggest themselves, but developing a plausible answer on Kant's behalf is a difficult business. What one seeks here is a criterion of moral relevance.
Kant claimed that when I tell a lie, I cannot will my maxim to become a universal law. I consider a situation in which the only way I can help someone in serious difficulty is by lying. Here two duties supposedly derivable from the same principle conflict with each other. Kant's discussion of this particular conflict is notoriously implausible. (See Kant, "On a Supposed Right to Tell Lies from Benevolent Motives," in *Kant's Critique of Practical Reason and Other Works on the Theory of Ethics*, ed. and trans. T. K. Abbott [London: Longmans, Green, 1909].) The distinction between "perfect" and "imperfect" duties, together with the claim that the former always take precedence over the latter is an unpromising basis for an account of how conflicts between duties are properly resolved. Several problems for Kant's moral philosophy intersect at this point.
2. Ruth Barcan Marcus, "Moral Dilemmas and Moral Consistency", *Journal of Philosophy* 77 (1980), 125.

consideration view that apparently precludes conflicts. In a particular situation, each of two contrary alternative courses of action may promote utility, but this does not create a conflict for utilitarians. Their principle does not tell them to promote utility wherever the opportunity presents itself; the principle prescribes *maximizing* utility. Utility is quantifiable wherever it occurs. The only consideration that indicates acting is that an act is reasonably expected to produce *more* utility than any alternative. If two contrary alternative acts will produce equal amounts of utility, the choice between them is morally indifferent. That a possible act will produce more utility than any alternatives is always a relevant consideration; on this view, there are no other candidates for the status of relevant consideration.

The ease with which this sort of utilitarianism avoids difficulties with relevance and conflict problems is a very attractive feature of the view, and some people are drawn to the theory despite the fact that the claim that there is but one overriding moral consideration contradicts appearances—that is, there do seem to be many different such considerations. For one thing, if one surveys the arguments of serious individuals for their positions on such vexed moral issues as disarmament, the insanity defense in the criminal law, and infanticide for neonates with severe defects, a great many different considerations appear to be involved. Stuart Hampshire's general observation is an eloquent description of how things seem.

> The ways of life which men aspire to and admire and wish
> to enjoy are normally a balance between, and combination of,
> disparate elements; and this is so, partly because human beings
> are not so constructed that they have just one overriding con-
> cern or end, one overriding interest, or even a few overriding
> desires and interests. They find themselves trying to reconcile,
> and to assign priorities to, widely different and diverging and

[11]

changing concerns and interests, both within the single life of an individual, and within a single society.[3]

Yet despite the fact that there appear to be many different moral considerations, the advantages of a single-consideration theory such as utilitarianism make such views highly attractive. Although the various versions of utilitarianism seem in a number of ways a bad fit with generally accepted moral beliefs and practices, these existing beliefs and practices are by no means beyond criticism. It is thus possible for utilitarians to fault the data rather than their theories for certain discrepancies. The appeal of utilitarianism lies in its promise to provide for the humane, tough-minded individual a way of resolving complex moral problems and disagreements by rational means. All considerations involved in a problem can be reduced to a single consideration that is sufficiently quantifiable to make possible direct comparisons of the quantity of good to be expected as the outcome of each alternative. Utilitarianism has its difficulties, but if one accepts the view that there is in the last analysis but one relevant good and that this comes in quanta, the conclusion that the best thing to do is to produce as much of it as possible is irresistible. The notion that goods are irreducibly multiple, on the other hand, seems to the utilitarian to entail the existence of moral conflict that is irresolvable by rational means. When irreducibly different moral considerations conflict, there is apparently no way rationally and objectively to compare, weigh, and balance them against one another to determine which is properly more compelling. It is the view that conflicts between irreducibly different moral considerations cannot be resolved by rational means, together with the con-

3. Stuart Hampshire, *Two Theories of Morality* (Oxford: Oxford University Press, 1977), pp. 17–18. See also Charles Taylor, "The Diversity of Goods," in Amartya Sen and Bernard Williams, eds., *Utilitarianism and Beyond* (Cambridge: Cambridge University Press, 1982), pp. 129–144.

viction that a morality worthy of an intelligent person's respect and allegiance must offer the possibility of reasoned solutions to problems and disagreements, that underlies the adherence of many people to utilitarianism.

Utilitarianism is criticized on a variety of grounds; it is a beleaguered theory. Critics argue that various versions of utilitarianism fail to square in too many ways with existing practices and beliefs. The ingenious and often complicated devices used by utilitarians to bring their theories more into harmony with the data often seem ad hoc and unconvincing. Particularly troubling to many is the fear that utilitarianism advocates abandoning certain precious goods when the consequences of so doing will maximize utility. So, it is feared, such things as the murder of the innocent, the betrayal of friends, and the commission of injustices will be justified in the eyes of utilitarians when by such means the general welfare can be increased.[4]

Modifications in classical act-utilitarianism designed to make the view less incongruous with actual moral beliefs may have the result that the revised view can no longer give the classical utilitarian answer to the question of how conflict problems are properly resolved. It has been suggested recently that we can retain the principle that we should maximize overall good, while allowing the possibility of a plurality of irreducibly different goods. It is also proposed that this revised view, a form of "consequentialism," should allow that there are certain constraints upon this principle that enable us to take into account how good is distributed and to pursue projects other than max-

---

4. See for example Alan Donagan, "Is There a Credible Form of Utilitarianism?", and H. J. McCloskey, "A Non-Utilitarian Approach to Punishment," in Michael D. Bayles, ed., *Contemporary Utilitarianism* (Garden City, N.Y.: Doubleday, 1968). See also John Rawls, *A Theory of Justice* (Cambridge: Harvard University Press, 1971), pp. 14, 22–27, and Bernard Williams, "A Critique of Utilitarianism," in J. J. C. Smart and B. Williams, *Utilitarianism: For and Against* (Cambridge: Cambridge University Press, 1973).

imizing the overall good in certain circumstances.[5] The utilitarian who abandons the classical view to move to such a position pays a price. The revised view can no longer offer the utilitarian response to the question of how conflict problems are properly resolved. What is relinquished here is one of the most attractive features of utilitarianism. It is not clear, moreover, how this revised view will deal with conflicts between the various different considerations it recognizes.

THE OBVIOUS theoretical means of guarding against the possibility of the unwelcome results of utilitarianism which its critics fear is to lay down a number of different principles that explicitly prohibit such outcomes. These principles might be given one of several different philosophical bases. In the context of a broadly utilitarian view, these principles might be thought to be justifiable by reference to a single, quantifiable good. The result would be rule-utilitarianism. On the other hand, those several principles might be given a deontological basis, or they might be thought of as protecting a variety of irreducibly different goods.[6]

However we conceive the basis of these several principles designed to guard against the possible unwelcome results of act-utilitarianism, it is clear that by adopting such principles we are committed to recognizing a multiplicity of different practical considerations. How, in particular cases, are we to establish the relevance of such considerations, and how are we to resolve conflicts among them?

5. See Samuel Scheffler, *The Rejection of Consequentialism* (Oxford: Clarendon Press, 1982), for a discussion of such a view.

6. For a brief discussion of the distinction between act- and rule-utilitarianism, with further references, see J. J. C. Smart and Bernard Williams, *Utilitarianism: For and Against*, pp. 9–12. For an example of a multiple-principle deontological theory, see John Finnis, *Natural Law and Natural Rights* (Oxford: Clarendon Press, 1980).

It may seem that a rule-utilitarian can have recourse to the principle of utility to resolve relevance and conflict problems: A consideration is to be relevant in a particular case just in case utility is maximized by taking it into account; when two considerations are in conflict, the principle of utility is used to determine what to do. When we consider, however, that the rule-utilitarian adopts those several principles in the hope that certain foreseen unwelcome results of the use of the principle of utility will be forestalled, the use of the utilitarian principle in this way to solve relevance and conflict problems is seen to be at odds with the rule-utilitarian enterprise. It is not surprising that some rule-utilitarians look to other means to explain how relevance and conflict problems are properly resolved.[7]

A common response from perspectives that recognize many considerations to the question of how relevance and conflict problems are properly resolved is to deny, in effect, that such problems occur. So, for example, it might be held that morality consists in a collection of hard-and-fast rules, which are actually very complicated, with a great many conditions and exceptions built into them. Thus, many cases that appear to engender a conflict of rules would turn out upon scrutiny to be cases in which one (or more) of the apparently conflicting rules does not apply, because of an exception built into the rule itself. On this view, what I describe as the ubiquity of situations posing relevance and conflict problems is to be understood as the way things appear to one who has a vague and crude conception of moral rules. A more precise and sophisticated understanding — one that has the rules right in all their complexity — will enable one to see that it is clear when the rules are and are not relevant and that the rules actually do not conflict in such cases. Another related view holds that the rules of morality are ranked in order of precedence, so if two

---

7. See, for example, R. B. Brandt, *A Theory of the Good and the Right* (Oxford: Clarendon Press, 1979), pp. 286–296.

rules do conflict in a particular case, the higher-ranking rule takes precedence.[8]

Attempts to articulate unexceptionable moral rules or systems of hard-and-fast moral principles ranked in order of precedence have not to date met with notable success. This by itself does not show that such programs are unfeasible. It is appropriate, however, to ask the proponents of such programs how we are to know when they have succeeded in producing correct (valid, true) formulations of unexceptionable moral principles. How is one to know that *this* particular set of principles, applied in an invariant order, will always, in every circumstance, prescribe exactly what one should do? If the principles in question are many and complicated, these questions will be especially troublesome. That a principle strikes one upon reflection as being in accord with one's experience and one's understanding of morality — that the principle accords with one's intuitions (however 'intuition' is understood) — does not establish that the principle really is correct. Someone with a lively sense of the complexity of practical affairs and an appreciation of his or her own fallibility in judgment will not confidently accept the claim that a certain set of complicated practical principles is correct solely on the grounds that on reflection the principles seem correct. It does not take much reflection on the extent and depth of disagreement among people on moral matters to convince us that there is no reasonable hope for a consensus that a given complicated set of moral principles invariably gives the correct result in concrete situations.

One response to the difficulty of establishing that a particular set of many complicated moral principles is correct is to attempt to show that these many principles can be deduced from a very few general principles that are thought to be fundamental. Different theorists favor different fundamental prin-

8. For a discussion of this theoretical device, see Rawls, *A Theory of Justice*, pp. 40–45.

ciples, and, again, there is little progress toward agreement in this enterprise. Lack of unqualified success so far is not a conclusive argument against the feasibility of such programs, but we might turn the question around and ask what reason there is to suppose that such a program can succeed. Underlying these efforts, often, is the assumption that moral principles form a deductive system. This is an extraordinary assumption. Why should it be supposed that our knowledge of what ought to be, unlike our knowledge of what is, takes the form of a mathematical system? Why should we be Pythagoreans in ethical theory?[9]

The thesis that most or all conflicts of moral considerations are only apparent because moral principles have an invariant order of precedence or because unexceptionable moral principles have enough conditions built into them that they do not conflict, involves the assumption that all soluble moral problems are, in the principles of morality themselves, decided in advance. How could a set of practical principles anticipate the continual and extensive changes in the human condition? Only *very general* principles could, with any plausibility at all, be said to apply in all of the diverse cultural and physical circumstances that have obtained throughout human history. But these are not the sort of principles envisioned by the absolutist. Someone who claims to have discovered such principles as the absolutist requires is claiming to have found principles that auto-

9. In the course of criticizing certain arguments for the thesis that there must exist very general exceptionless moral principles, J. B. Schneewind points out that some of these arguments depend upon the assumption that "the reasoning needed in morality is purely deductive." Schneewind makes the point that it is possible to construe moral principles and their inferential relations to one another on other models than that of axioms in a deductive system. See "Moral Knowledge and Moral Principles," *Knowledge and Necessity*, Royal Institute of Philosophy Lectures 3 (1968-69), 249-262. This essay is reprinted in Stanley Hauerwas and Alasdair MacIntyre, eds., *Revisions: Changing Perspectives in Moral Philosophy* (Notre Dame: University of Notre Dame Press, 1983), pp. 113-126.

matically provide the correct solution for every soluble moral problem, past, present, and future. How could anyone have sufficient grounds for such a claim?[10]

THE TAXONOMY or classification of philosophical theories is a difficult business, and it is unfortunately apt to lead to misunderstanding and confusion rather than illumination. I am embarked upon this, however, and I want to be as clear as possible. I have distinguished two types of views, common in moral theories, that pertain to the question of how conflicts among considerations are properly resolved. I will call these the "Utilitarian Response" and the "Absolutist Response" to this question. These are natural labels to use for a distinction I make for a philosophical purpose. It is important to bear in mind, however, that not every moral theory that might be classified as a utilitarian moral theory offers what I call the Utilitarian Response to the question of how to resolve conflicts.

I want to distinguish kinds of responses by moral theorists to the following question:

Q. In a concrete practical problem, when one relevant consideration indicates one course of action and other relevant considerations indicate contrary courses, how does one properly determine which consideration(s) is (are) decisive—i.e., which course of action is supported by the strongest reasons?

In brief, what I call the Utilitarian Response to Q is:

In any practical problem, there is but one relevant consideration, utility, and utility comes in quanta. The course of action that is reasonably expected to result in the most utility—more

10. On this point see Arthur E. Murphy, *The Theory of Practical Reason* (La Salle, Ill.: Open Court, 1967), pp. 206-208.

[18]

utility than any of the alternatives—is the course of action indicated by the strongest reason.

What I call the Absolutist Response is, briefly:

> There exists a variety of irreducibly different practical considerations. These considerations, however, properly understood, never conflict with one another in actual practical problems. The problem described in Q never really arises.

Here, then, are two ways in which ethical theorists respond to the question, what should a reasonable person of good will do in a situation in which relevant considerations indicate contrary courses of action? Both responses rest upon the assumptions that (1) *genuine* conflicts between irreducibly different moral considerations could not be resolved by rational means, and (2) all or most moral problems can (in principle) be solved by rational means. Both responses claim that vexing moral problems that appear to involve conflicts really do not—that on a closer scrutiny of the considerations, the conflict disappears. Both ways of dealing with these problems involve such profound difficulties and are open to such serious objections that a search for a viable alternative is indicated.

When struck by the multiplicity of different practical considerations and the implausibility of the idea that there exist ready-made, hard-and-fast rules that in every case tell us the right thing to do, we may be tempted by what I will call the "Intuitionist Response"—the account of how to deal with conflict problems that was defended by W. D. Ross.[11] On this view, there exist many moral considerations that may at times be in genuine conflict with one another. The determination of which considerations should yield when two or more considerations conflict is not governed by any rule or principle. That

11. W.D. Ross, *The Right and the Good* (Oxford: Clarendon Press, 1930), chap. 2.

certain things are in general moral considerations is, on this view, self-evident. Reasonable, well-brought-up individuals are able to judge in particular cases which considerations are decisive, although no general principle can be cited to justify the judgment and no general account can be given of how this properly is done. This, then, is the Intuitionist Response to Q:

> There exists a variety of irreducibly different considerations that do come into conflict with one another in practical problems. There are no general principles that indicate which considerations prevail in these problems, and no general account can be given of how properly to determine which considerations prevail. It is possible, however, to judge or intuit *correctly* which considerations are the stronger in a particular situation.

This view, however, provides only the appearance of an account of how conflict problems are properly resolved. One simply judges or intuits on such a view which consideration properly is decisive. No basis is provided for distinguishing between arbitrarily declaring a consideration decisive and correctly judging it decisive. This view is in the end indistinguishable from the view that genuine conflict problems are not resolvable by rational means.[12]

Not every intuitionist moral theory offers the Intuitionist Response to Q. Intuitionist *theories* are characterized by their appeal at crucial points to the self-evidence of certain claims. They maintain that certain things are known to be true independently of any external evidence or any argument. Certain truths, on such theories, proclaim their truth directly to the understanding. So an intuitionist theorist might hold that a number of different moral principles are self-evident, but give the Absolutist Response to the question of what to do if such moral principles conflict.

12. This is the conclusion of D. D. Raphael in "The Standard of Morals," *Proceedings of the Aristotelian Society* 75 (1974–75), 1–12.

The Intuitionist Response to the problem of conflicting considerations has seemed attractive to moral theorists who are impressed by the difficulties with the Utilitarian and Absolutist Responses. Thus Ross offers his account as one that fits the facts better than either "Kant's view" (interpreted as offering the Absolutist Response) or the utilitarian views of "Professor Moore and Dr. Rashdall."[13] J. O. Urmson concludes an article entitled "A Defense of Intuitionism" with these words.

> If it be recognized that there is a plurality of primary moral reasons for action, the complexity of many situations seems to me to make it implausible to suppose that we are guided (presumably unwittingly) by any decision-procedure when we weigh up the pros and cons. I also doubt whether our moral beliefs have the internal harmony requisite for a decision-procedure to be even theoretically possible. This leaves us with the need for an intuitive weighing up of reasons; since this seems to be not an irrational anomaly but our ordinary predicament with regard to reasons in most fields, I find this conclusion neither surprising nor unduly distressing.[14]

There is something to be said for the claims of Ross and Urmson that their account is more congruent with what actually goes on in the practical thinking of reasonable people than the accounts employing the Utilitarian and Absolutist Responses. Actual practice is far too complex to be accommodated to the simple picture offered by the latter accounts. The response that actual practice is confused and inconsistent might have force if either of these latter accounts seemed adequate on its own. When one considers the serious philosophical difficulties that beset these views, however, this response is weak. In the mood generated by these reflections, the Intuitionist Response

13. Ross, *The Right and the Good*, pp. 17–19.
14. J. O. Urmson, "A Defense of Intuitionism," *Proceedings of the Aristotelian Society* 75 (1974–75), 119.

can be tempting.[15] Yet the accounts offering the Intuitionist Response are in a crucial respect perilously thin. What, on these views, is the difference between "intuitively weighing reasons for and against" and *arbitrarily* selecting one reason over another? What is the standard for doing such weighing *correctly*? Unless there are answers to such questions, a remark made by Ludwig Wittgenstein, in a different but related context, is apt: "In the present case I have no criterion of correctness. One would like to say: Whatever is going to seem right to me is right. And that only means that here we can't talk about 'right'."[16]

It is not by oversight that the proponents of the Intuitionist Response provide no answer to the question of how one distinguishes between correct and incorrect determinations of which reason is stronger. The matter looks this way to the proponent of the Intuitionist Response: If an argument could be produced to *make a case* for the superiority of one solution to a conflict problem over another, the argument must involve an appeal to one or more *general considerations* or *principles* that imply that one of the conflicting considerations takes precedence over the others. If we allow the existence of such general principle(s), however, the Intuitionist believes, we find ourselves in the end embracing either the Absolutist Response or the Utilitarian Response.

If the possible views about how conflict problems are properly resolved are exhausted by the Intuitionist, the Absolutist, and the Utilitarian Response, and if (as seems to be the case) none of these views is satisfactory, then we must conclude that solutions to conflict problems cannot be defended before the court of reason. This conclusion, given the ubiquity and impor-

15. For a discussion of the conception of reasoning in the views of Raphael and Urmson, see Frederick L. Will, "Pragmatic Rationality," *Philosophical Investigations* 8 (1985), 120–142.

16. Ludwig Wittgenstein, *Philosophical Investigations*, trans. G. E. M. Anscombe (New York: Macmillan, 1953), Part I, Sec. 258, p. 92e.

tance of conflict problems in our lives, would constitute a significant victory for skepticism and irrationalism. It is worth considering, then, why these three responses seem the only possible answers to question Q and inquiring whether there might not be other, better responses.

[2]

The Passive Conception
of Practical Reasoning

HENRY SIDGWICK appreciated the importance of relevance and conflict problems. Throughout the long and complicated argument of his book *The Methods of Ethics*, the question of how such problems are properly resolved is prominent.[1] The difficulty of this question defeated Sidgwick in the end. His failure to find a way to resolve conflicts he saw between what he took to be fundamental ethical principles was catastrophic for his own theory, and he admitted as much. His exploration of the issues involved, however, is admirable for its thoroughness and critical acumen. Unintentionally, Sidgwick made a strong case for abandoning certain of his own assumptions about practical reasoning. These same assumptions, which are plausible and widely held, contribute substantially to the impression that the only possible accounts of how relevance and conflict problems are properly resolved are the Absolutist, the Intuitionist, and

---

1. *The Methods of Ethics* was first published in 1874. It was revised a number of times, the seventh and final edition being published in 1907. Unless otherwise indicated, numbers in parentheses in the text refer to pages in Henry Sidgwick, *The Methods of Ethics*, 7th ed. (London: Macmillan, 1907).

[24]

the Utilitarian Responses. An examination of certain of Sidgwick's views is useful for understanding these assumptions and their consequences.

SIDGWICK WROTE:

> When I am asked, "Do you not consider it ultimately reasonable to seek pleasure and avoid pain for yourself?" "Have you not a moral sense?" "Do you not intuitively pronounce some actions to be right and others wrong?" "Do you not acknowledge the general happiness to be a paramount end?" I answer 'yes' to all these questions. My difficulty begins when I have to choose between the different principles or inferences drawn from them. We admit the necessity, when they conflict, of making this choice, and that it is irrational to let sometimes one principle prevail and sometimes another; but the necessity is a painful one. We cannot but hope that all methods may ultimately coincide: And at any rate, before making our election we may reasonably wish to have the completest possible knowledge of each. [14]

Each of the questions in this passage alludes to what Sidgwick calls a "method of ethics" — a rational procedure by which individuals determine what they ought to do, a procedure whose use is thought to be incumbent upon individuals regardless of their particular desires and goals (6–8). The method that adopts as the ultimate end the agent's own happiness and makes the criterion of right action whatever maximizes the agent's happiness, Sidgwick calls the "method of egoistic hedonism." The "method of utilitarianism" is similar except that the *general* happiness is adopted as the ultimate end. A third method, the "method of intuitionism," in one version takes the criterion of right reason to be conformity to certain moral principles that are seen intuitively to be binding upon us. Each of these methods, according to Sidgwick, considered by itself, appears paradigmatic of rational procedure in practical thinking. The difficulty lies in understanding the relation of these methods to one another.

For each of these methods, Sidgwick finds a philosophical theory whose name corresponds—egoism, utilitarianism, and intuitionism. Each theory takes its corresponding method as ultimately the only proper way to determine right action, and each theory denies the claims of the other two methods to be ultimate. In *The Methods of Ethics*, Sidgwick examines in turn each of these three methods and at the same time examines the philosophical theory that takes the method to be *the* way of reaching well-founded convictions about right action. Sidgwick's ultimate conclusion is that there is something right in all three methods. A person errs in some important respect in altogether rejecting any of them. The philosophical *theory* that takes the method of intuitionism to be the sole determinant of right action is totally inadequate, Sidgwick argues. It fails on its own grounds. The *method* of intuitionism, on the other hand, when it is the rules of "the morality of common sense" that are intuited, coincides rather closely in its results with the method of utilitarianism. The precepts of common-sense morality, Sidgwick maintained, have a utilitarian basis—they are (imperfect) guidelines for promoting the general happiness. Thus, Sidgwick found, the rationality of supporting and (for the most part) following these precepts—in other words, the rationality of the method of intuitionism—can be accounted for by the *philosophical theory* of utilitarianism. In most cases, Sidgwick argued, individuals are more apt to promote the general happiness by following these maxims than by attempting to determine in each case what action is most apt to maximize the general happiness. Common-sense morality is also dependent upon utilitarian considerations in that, in actual practice, when moral maxims conflict or when their application is unclear, the general-happiness principle is appealed to as the method of choice (421–422). There remains, according to Sidgwick, a class of cases in which, by the method of utilitarianism, a certain action is right and, according to the morality of common sense, that action is wrong — cases in which the methods of utilitarianism and intuitionism conflict. Sidgwick was relatively unperturbed by this result. The philosophical case for regarding the maxims of common-sense morality as the ultimate standards of rationality in the practical sphere had been examined and found unsatisfactory. Sidgwick was profoundly troubled, however, by the many apparent conflicts between the method of "egoistic hedonism" on the one hand and the methods of utilitarianism and intuitionism on the other. In many cases, both the utilitarian principle and the maxims of common-sense morality appear to require individuals to sacrifice their interests. Sidgwick could find no decisive argument against the philosophical claim that the method of egoism is the ultimate determinant of rationality in the practical sphere. He thought that these conflicts could be resolved only by supposing that there is an afterlife in which sacrifices of one's interests in the name of duty are rewarded and selfish vice punished. Sidgwick could see no independent grounds for this supposition. He was constrained in the end to admit that it is possible that there is a "fundamental contradiction in our apparent intuitions of what is reasonable in conduct." If there exists such a contradiction, then "it would seem to follow that the apparently intuitive operation of the Practical Reason, manifested in these contradictory judgments, is after all illusory" (508). In other words it would seem to follow from such a contradiction that our belief that we are following the dictates of reason in employing the standard methods of ethics is mistaken.[2]

2. Sidgwick said (p. 6) "We cannot, of course, regard as valid reasonings that lead to conflicting conclusions; and I therefore assume as a fundamental postulate of Ethics, that so far as two methods conflict, one or other of them must be modified or rejected." He said (p. 12) that it is "a postulate of Practical Reason, that two conflicting rules of action cannot both be reasonable."

THE LAST argument might be reconstructed in this way. The following precepts underlie the practice of serious people and would be acknowledged by them upon reflection to be intuitively certain.

(1) Reason requires us to pursue our own interests.
(2) Reason requires us to produce as much good on the whole as possible.

Situations arise in which it appears that we can produce the greatest amount of good on the whole only by sacrificing our own interests. If things really are as they appear in these situations, then we must conclude that our apparent intuitions of what is reasonable in the practical sphere are not to be trusted.

This argument, as I have set it out, is an enthymeme, but the missing premises can be found in *The Methods of Ethics*. Among these missing premises are the assumptions that lead to an impasse in the search for understanding how relevance and conflict problems are properly resolved.

The disconcerting conclusion of the argument might have been foreseen by Sidgwick if he had generalized his own criticisms of the philosophical theory he called "dogmatic intuitionism". According to this theory, the many maxims of common-sense morality are the ultimate determinants of practical rationality, and these maxims are known to be so by intuition. Sidgwick showed, in effect, that on such a theory, relevance and conflict problems are insoluble. Practical reasoning becomes impossible in just those instances where it is most needed; its claims to be a guide to conduct are not upheld on this view. Sidgwick is successful in this criticism, I think. Sidgwick maintained, however, that the principle one follows on the utilitarian method is itself known by intuition to be a demand of rationality. (Strictly it is deduced from two other principles and a hedonistic theory of value that are warranted by intuition. See note 6 below.) The principle of the method of egoism is known by intuition, according to Sidgwick. Conflicts between those two principles, therefore, as Sidgwick conceived these principles, are analogous to conflicts between moral maxims conceived as dogmatic intuitionists conceived them. Sidgwick showed that the latter conflicts are intractable—they do not admit of resolution by rational means.

I WANT to examine briefly Sidgwick's criticisms of the theory of dogmatic intuitionism. The difficulties that he found with this view have very general implications for the theory of practical reason. The lesson to be learned here is that in order to understand how relevance and conflict problems are to be resolved by rational means, we must abandon certain assumptions shared by Sidgwick and the dogmatic intuitionist, assumptions that have been and are widely held.

The relevant moral theory of intuitionism—Sidgwick distinguishes several kinds of intuitionism (100–103)—holds that:

> We can discern certain general rules with really clear and finally valid intuition. It is held that such general rules are implicit in the moral reasoning of ordinary men, who apprehend them adequately for most practical purposes, and are able to enunciate them roughly; but that to state them with proper precision requires a special habit of contemplating clearly and steadily abstract moral notions. It is held that the moralist's function then is to perform this process of abstract contemplation, to arrange the results as systematically as possible, and by proper definitions and explanations to remove vagueness and prevent conflict. [101]

This is "the view of ethics which regards as the practically ultimate end of moral actions their conformity to certain rules or dictates of duty unconditionally prescribed" (96). The "certain rules" are moral rules implicit in the practice and reasoning of ordinary men and women; they are the rules we appeal to when we use the intuitional method to determine what we ought

[29]

to do. This *theory* takes the *method* of intuitionism to be the *only* proper way to determine how we morally should act. The rules are ultimate, and they are closely related to the actual moral beliefs and practices of ordinary people.

The method of intuitionism, according to Sidgwick, involves the exercise of our capacity to see that certain particular actions are wrong. Certain particular actions — for example, certain actions involving cheating, breaking faith, violating confidences, or betraying friends — seem to us wrong in themselves. Sidgwick remarks that it would be paradoxical to deny this phenomenon in the conscious experience of mankind. Such "intuitions" are not infallible, as shown by the fact that we sometimes find that our intuitions on one occasion are inconsistent with those on another occasion (210–211). We may seek to correct these particular intuitions, however, by discovering valid general rules according to which *kinds* of acts are wrong in themselves — cheating, violating confidences, and the like (200). We can in fact find a set of rules whose validity is admitted by members of our community "which would cover with approximate completeness the whole of human conduct" (215). Those rules comprise what Sidgwick called "the morality of Common Sense." Those rules, however, are not always clear and precise enough to enable us to decide the cases that we need to decide.

> We shall probably all accept the general maxims, that 'we ought to give every man his own' and that 'we ought to speak the truth': but when we ask (1) whether primogeniture is just, or the disendowment of corporations, or the determination of the value of services by competition, or (2) whether and how far false statements may be allowed in speeches of advocates, or in religious ceremonials, or when made to enemies or robbers, or in defense of lawful secrets, we do not find that these or any other current maxims enable us to give clear and unhesitating decisions. And yet such particular questions are, after all, those to which we naturally expect answers from the moralist. [215]

[30]

If the method of intuitionism is to serve as *the sole way* of making well-founded moral judgments (as it must on the theory of dogmatic intuitionism), and if we hope to solve the moral problems that vex us, we cannot be satisfied with the vagueness of the rules of common-sense morality. It is therefore part of the program of the theory of dogmatic intuitionism to systematize and make more definite and precise the rules implicit in our moral reasoning so that we "remove vagueness and prevent conflict" (101, 215–216).

It is also a central tenet of dogmatic intuitionism that when the axioms of common-sense morality have been raised to the proper degree of preciseness and made consistent with one another, it will be found that "their truth is self-evident, and must be accepted at once by an intelligent and unbiased mind" (229). If one is to establish "a proposition, apparently self-evident, in the highest degree of certainty attainable," Sidgwick maintained, four conditions must be fulfilled: (1) The terms of the proposition must be clear and precise. (2) The self-evidence of the proposition must be ascertained by careful reflection. (3) The propositions accepted as self-evident must be mutually consistent. (4) Others must not deny the proposition (338–342).

Sidgwick's examination of the theory of dogmatic intuitionism and the method of intuitionism consists in studies of various "areas" of morality or "departments of duty" such as benevolence, justice, and veracity, to see if in fact it is reasonable to suppose that there are such self-evident ethical axioms implicit in common-sense morality. Sidgwick found in many areas that the morality of common sense had no definite position at all on certain important questions. When it did seem plausible to suppose that common sense recognized a self-evident axiom, the axiom invariably lacked the degree of preciseness and definiteness required by the theory of dogmatic intuitionism. When these same putative axioms are made more precise and definite, Sidgwick found that they lose their apparent self-evidence (342–343). After examining many examples drawn from a variety of moral contexts, Sidgwick concluded that there cannot be found implicit in the morality of common sense the sort of ethical axioms required by dogmatic intuitionism.

Sidgwick's criticisms strike at the very heart of this theory. The requirement of dogmatic intuitionism that the self-evident axioms be definite, clear, and "consistent" is no mere embellishment. On the intuitionist conception Sidgwick examines, the set of ethical axioms is the only recourse in developing well-founded moral judgments. Rationality in moral matters, on this view, *consists in* consulting these rules and doing as they direct. On this view, for every decidable moral question there must be a rule in the system that unambiguously covers the case. The set of rules or axioms the intuitionist seeks must be complete in this sense. Sidgwick found that the requirement that the putative axioms be definite, precise, and consistent tended to clash with the requirement that the axioms be self-evident. He found over and over that the putative axioms with a plausible claim to self-evidence are "vague" — they do not decide certain crucial hard cases. When these axioms are made definite and precise so that they decide these hard cases, the revised versions no longer meet the conditions for self-evidence.

This last result is not difficult to understand. The interesting and important problems that are the hard cases are, of course, cases that puzzle us. These are situations in which we are uncertain about what should be done or where people disagree about what should be done. If we take a rule that seems to us correct and reformulate it so that the revised rule yields a definite result in a disputed or vexed case, we should expect that whatever doubts or disagreements we have about the case will transfer themselves to the reformulated rule. The *only* ground for the correctness of the revised rule is its self-evidence, which is determined by the rule's seeming self-evident and by individuals' agreeing that it seems self-evident. The existence of cases in which we are genuinely uncertain about what should be done or in which we disagree about what should be done,

[32]

cases that are covered by the revised rule in such a way that the rule unambiguously indicates what should be done, will undermine the rule's claim to self-evidence.

Sidgwick offers a great many examples of putative ethical axioms that turn out not to meet the requirements of dogmatic intuitionism. For instance, we are inclined to agree at first that we have a duty to fulfill express promises and distinct under-standings — that this proposition is self-evident. There are, how-ever, hard cases: promises made under various forms of duress, promises in which the promisor was misled in some material way by the promisee (either intentionally or unintentionally), and cases in which certain conditions that are not explicit con-ditions of an express promise change after the promise is made.[3] Among the cases that fit these descriptions are many in which individuals are genuinely uncertain whether the promi-sor is bound to keep an express promise and some in which individuals disagree about whether the promisor is duty-bound to perform. When such cases are brought to our attention, we will conclude that we were mistaken in supposing the original axiom to be self-evident. Moreover, the project of reformulat-ing this proposition so that it excludes the express promises that are *not* binding and applies to all and only binding express promises is not going to succeed if our aim is to meet the requirements of dogmatic intuitionism. We might agree that the proposition that we have a duty to fulfill express promises *when these are binding* is a self-evident ethical axiom. This for-mulation, however, is vague and imprecise in just the way that makes it unsatisfactory for the purposes of dogmatic intuition-ism. If this is all that reason can offer on the subject of our duty with respect to express promises, then we will be unable to determine what we should do in cases where it is unclear to

3. For a discussion of some hard cases involving promises see W. D. Ross, *Foundations of Ethics* (Oxford: Clarendon Press, 1939), chap. 5, pp. 87–113.

us or controversial whether a promise is binding. If we attempt to make the axiom more precise and definite by giving an account of when express promises are binding, and if our only criterion of having completed our task correctly is the self-evidence of the resulting formulation, then we are bound to fail. The existence of hard cases in which it is unclear or controversial whether an express promise is binding will undermine the claim to self-evidence of any more definite and precise axiom. Thus, the existence of hard cases dooms to failure the enterprise of dogmatic intuitionism (303–311, 353–354).

The intuitionist must also insist that the set of self-evident ethical axioms gives at most one answer to any question of the form, what ought to be done in such and such a case? Rules that give conflicting answers will not serve as guides to action — these rules are, according to dogmatic intuitionism, the sole determinants of what we should do. These self-evident ethical axioms, then, must be in this sense consistent. Sidgwick exhibits cases in which rules of common-sense morality that seem self-evident conflict with one another. For example, one's parent asks for one's help in escaping punishment for a crime. In certain cases of this sort, reflective individuals will disagree about whether one should help one's parent. The duty of "law-observance" is in such cases in conflict with "the duties of domestic relations" (302). If one is genuinely torn over whether one should help a parent in such a case, or if people disagree about whether one should help, then any reformulation of the rules of law-observance and the rules of domestic relations that will resolve this conflict will result in at least one rule whose claim to self-evidence cannot be sustained. In this and other cases, Sidgwick found that rules of common-sense morality that seem to us correct actually conflict. When one or more rules are amended to resolve the conflict, the uncertainty or controversy surrounding the case transfers itself to one or another of the revised rules, and the rule or rules lose their claim to self-evidence (302).

Sidgwick argued in this way that we cannot find a system of rules implicit in common-sense morality that satisfies both the following requirements: (1) The rules are so precise and consistent that conflict and relevance problems do not arise in their application. (2) Each rule seems to us upon reflection to be obviously correct. Sidgwick found, after a survey of the morality of common sense, that its maxims are often problematic: we are accustomed to hard cases in which either it is unclear whether a maxim applies or where conflicting maxims seem applicable. The dogmatic intuitionist's program is based upon the hope that there is some version of the maxims of common-sense morality for which there are no hard cases, that this is the true morality, and that this set properly commands our allegiance and provides grounds for correct judgments about what ought to be done. Sidgwick examined in some detail certain areas of morality, certain ranges of moral questions, to see if such rules could be found. The results of his search were negative in every area, and he concluded that there are no such rules.

SIDGWICK'S CRITICISM of the theory of dogmatic intuitionism is substantially a criticism of the Absolutist Response to relevance and conflict problems — not the Intuitionist Response. In employing the Absolutist Response, the theory of dogmatic intuitionism invests the rules of morality with extraordinary authority. These rules are the *sole* criteria of correctness and reasonableness in moral questions. We, moreover, insofar as we are rational beings, must be passive in our attitude toward these rules. The rules tell us what to do, and it is incumbent upon us as rational individuals simply to do as we are told. On this view, any departure from these rules, any quibbling with them, cannot be justifiable, because the rules themselves are definitive of correctness in moral matters and are the sole court of appeal in justification. The rules are conceived as sovereign and the rational agent as the passive obedient subject. It is the conception of morality as absolute rules directed to individuals who are passive with respect to them that lies behind the requirement of dogmatic intuitionism (and other theories subscribing to the Absolutist Response) that moral rules be *precise*, *definite*, and *consistent*. On this view, these rules are the only intellectual recourse in practical problems that have a moral dimension. There can be no such thing as a reasoned interpretation of a rule in a particular case or a justifiable judgment that one rule takes precedence over another in a particular case except insofar as such interpretations and judgments are explicitly sanctioned by the rules themselves. The rules of morality, on this conception, must do all the work for us.

A rule-intuitionist moral theory, such as "dogmatic intuitionism," is a natural concomitant of the Absolutist Response, since on such a view, not only are the rules self-interpreting and self-applying, but they are also self-certifying, self-evident. They are, on such a view, doubly autonomous. Other sorts of moral theories, of course, avail themselves of the Absolutist Response — rule-utilitarian and contractualist theories provide examples. On these theories, the rules of morality are justified by their tendencies to produce nonmoral good or by their serving the interests of individuals. For important reasons, however, the proponents of such theories wish to interpose a barrier between the considerations that justify moral rules and the considerations that determine what action to take in particular cases. They do this, of course, by insisting that the rules themselves are the sole determinants of right action. These theorists must resist the suggestion that relevance and conflict problems involving these rules are properly solved by considering which of the possible solutions most advances the considerations that justify the rules. It is important to them that such considerations not be available to justify the actions falling under the rules.[4] The rules alone must decide in every case what action to take — these must be the sole standard of right action. This, in essence, is the Absolutist Response.

It is the requirements of various moral *theories* that lead philosophers to embrace the Absolutist Response to the question of how moral relevance and conflict problems are properly resolved. The case for the existence of rules such as the Absolutist Response requires is in this respect a priori. If we look closely at the actual practice of serious, responsible individuals attempting to resolve real moral problems — as Sidgwick did in examining the claims of dogmatic intuitionism — it is apparent the actual practice is widely different from what would be the case if individuals proceeded as the Absolutist Response suggests.

Not only does the claim that there are such *rules* as the Absolutist Response requires get no support from cognitive practice, but it seems incongruous with such practice to suggest that rational agents are passive with respect to moral rules in the way implied by views that adopt this response. Being reasonable in moral matters, one would think, consists in more than merely doing what properly certified rules say. One who proceeds reasonably and intelligently in accordance with rules does not just passively and blindly follow the rules. The reasonable individual actively applies the rules to the problem at hand. This is an intellectual activity that itself can be done well or badly, intelligently or stupidly, reasonably or arbitrarily. Central to this activity are such intellectual tasks as determining whether a certain rule applies when this is problematic and resolving conflicts when rules conflict in particular cases. Obviously such intellectual tasks cannot be accounted for on the passive conception of rationality in practical affairs.

4. See John Rawls, "Two Concepts of Rules," *Philosophical Review* 64 (1955), 3–32.

If we adhere to the passive conception, and if we hold that corresponding to the maxims of common-sense morality, there are "axioms" that determine what we ought to do, then these assumptions will govern our response to the question of how relevance and conflict problems properly are resolved. The most attractive response, granting that relevance and conflict problems are common, is to blame these problems upon our failure to be clear about what the rules of morality really are. If these rules genuinely do determine what ought to be done, they must be precise enough to give the desired result and they must not conflict in particular cases. The remedy is to seek formulations of the rules of the morality of common sense that are sufficiently precise and consistent that conflict and relevance problems do not arise. The desired formulations will in every case tell us precisely and unequivocally what we ought to do. Being reasonable in practical matters will consist in doing what these rules say. In any actual case where these rules do not apply, there will be no well-founded answer to the question, what ought to be done? How will we recognize the correct formulations? One answer is: as rational beings, we will recognize the voice of reason when it speaks. The elaboration of this answer — such elaboration as it permits — is called intuitionism. Answers that appear more promising are that the correct formulations of the rules will maximize utility or are such that rational beings would choose to live under them in preference to other formulations. Now, plausible arguments can be produced for the claim that certain moral principles serve human needs and interests in important ways. This, however, is not the same thing as showing that a set of rules of the complexity required for the purposes of the Absolutist Response — rules that unambiguously tell us what to do in every circumstance — will produce more utility or would be preferable on certain grounds than alternative sets of rules of comparable complexity. No one has ever seriously attempted such a task, and for good reason. The task is beyond the powers of finite intellects.

[38]

SIDGWICK REJECTED the theory of dogmatic intuitionism on the grounds that the desired formulations of the maxims of common-sense morality are not to be found. Sidgwick's response to these results was not to give up the passive conception of rationality in following rules, nor was it to give up intuitionism. He himself clearly embraced both these views. He concluded from the failure of dogmatic intuitionism that it is necessary to abandon the idea that the maxims of common-sense morality, in some formulation or other, are the ultimate principles that determine what ought to be done.

Sidgwick found that the philosophical theory of utilitarianism — the view that maintains that the General-Happiness Principle (GHP) is the ultimate practical principle — provides an explanation of our attachment to the maxims of common-sense morality and a partial, qualified endorsement of the *method* of intuitionism. Moreover, Sidgwick claimed, when ordinary people encounter a problem where the relevance of a maxim of common-sense morality is unclear or where relevant maxims conflict, they commonly solve the problem by the use of the method of utilitarianism. The maxims of common-sense morality, according to Sidgwick, depend upon utilitarian considerations in two ways.

(1) In actual practice, the exceptions to the maxims are determined by the GHP, the vagueness of the maxims is made determinate by the use of the GHP, and conflicts among maxims are resolved by appeal to the GHP.

(2) The maxims of common-sense morality can be explained as a set of (imperfect) rules for promoting the general happiness. [421–422 and Book IV, chap. III]

Utilitarianism, introduced by Sidgwick after his discussion of dogmatic intuitionism, seems by contrast a most attractive view. The morality of common sense appears to be a hodgepodge of vague and conflicting maxims whose claim upon our allegiance is puzzling. Such maxims cannot possibly provide

[39]

the sort of guidance desired by a proponent of the passive conception. The utilitarian theory, by contrast, provides at once an account of the point of those maxims and explicit directions for their criticism and improvement. The view that the GHP is the sole ultimate practical principle and that the maxims of common-sense morality are secondary principles meant to promote the general happiness provides the rationale for a single method of resolving relevance and conflict problems. The method itself is intuitively plausible, apparently humane, and seems at least roughly consistent with actual practice in dealing with relevance and conflict problems. Some people doubt that the general happiness is the only consideration in properly resolving relevance and conflict problems, but the doctrine that it is the only consideration is a strength of the utilitarian position. If there were other considerations relevant to the proper resolution of conflicts, these other considerations might conflict with one another and with the GHP in particular cases, reintroducing the possibility of conflicts that do not admit of resolution by rational means.

Nonetheless, despite the theoretical advantages of utilitarianism over dogmatic intuitionism (and, generally, over theories employing the Absolutist Response), in fact, as Sidgwick presents it, utilitarianism is vulnerable to the same sorts of objections that he deployed against dogmatic intuitionism. When the GHP is confronted with certain sorts of important cases, it shows the same defects that Sidgwick found with the maxims of common-sense morality. Although he apparently was not aware of it, these difficulties with the GHP arise in his own discussions of utilitarianism.

CONSIDER, for example, Sidgwick's well-known discussion of the application of the GHP to problems about population policy (Book IV, chap. I, §2). Sidgwick noted that we can to some extent influence the future size of the population (414).

How, on utilitarian grounds, he asked, should this influence be exercised? If we assume that the average happiness of human beings is a positive quantity, and that the average happiness remains constant as the population increases, the GHP directs us to make the number enjoying this level of happiness as great as possible (415). Of course, the assumption that the average happiness of individuals would remain constant as the population increased indefinitely is implausible. At a certain point, further increase in the size of the population is bound to result in a decrease in the average level of happiness. This creates the interesting possibility that we might at some point have to choose between increasing the *sum* of general happiness by increasing the population or maintaining the *average* happiness at its present level by holding the size of the population in check.

Sidgwick thought it clear that faced with such a choice, we should aim at maximizing the sum of happiness — the "greatest good on the whole" — rather than aiming at the greatest average happiness. The GHP commits him to this view. "The conduct which, under any given circumstances, is objectively right," he wrote, "is that which will produce the greatest amount of happiness on the whole; that is, taking into account all whose happiness is affected by the conduct" (411).

However plausible this principle may seem in the abstract, when it is confronted with the problem of choosing between the greatest amount of happiness in sum or the greatest average happiness for individuals, one begins to have doubts. There is a certain prima facie plausibility to the claim that the GHP expresses the attitude of an individual who is both rational and benevolent, thus capturing the central concern of morality as we understand it.[5] Is it clear, however, that *benevolence* would

5. This claim is made by J. J. C. Smart, "An Outline of a System of Utilitarian Ethics," in Smart and Williams, *Utilitarianism: For and Against*, p. 7.

lead an individual to favor a large *sum* of happiness in the world when this must be purchased at the price of a lower level of happiness for individuals? The GHP here favors the maximization of a statistic at the expense of individuals' happiness, and it is not clear by any means that this would be favored by a benevolent individual.

This discussion is similar in important ways to Sidgwick's discussions of certain maxims of common-sense morality. One is initially inclined to agree, he maintained, that it is an axiom of morality that we have an obligation to keep our express promises. Certain hard cases, however, raise doubts about this. The maxim of promising, so formulated, no longer appears self-evident. Sidgwick, of course, does not simply claim that the GHP is self-evident. It is, rather, presented as a deduction from other principles that are claimed to be self-evident, combined with an account of "ultimate good" that he claims to intuit. The uncertainty of the GHP itself, however, should reflect upon one or more of the "axioms" from which it is deduced. In effect, Sidgwick argues (382) that both the following principles are self-evident:

(1) One ought to produce as much good as possible.
(2) Quantity of good is independent of its location — that is, of *whose* good it is.

From these principles, Sidgwick deduces the "maxim of Benevolence" which says, in effect, that one ought to view everyone's good impartially, taking into account only quantity of good, when one pursues the goal of producing as much good as possible.[6] All that is needed to reach the principle of utili-

6. On p. 382, Sidgwick states his two self-evident principles as follows:
(B1) "The good of any one individual is of no more importance, from the point of view . . . of the Universe, than the good of any other; unless, that is, there are special grounds for believing that more good is likely to be realized in the one case than in the other."

tarianism, the GHP, is the view that this good we are bound to produce as much of as possible is happiness (388–389 and Book III, chap. XIV).

A utilitarian who believes that the proper course, when one is forced to choose between maximizing the total sum of utility and maximizing the average utility, is to maximize the average is implicitly denying Sidgwick's principle that one is bound to produce "as much good as possible." Indeed, this sort of case casts doubt upon this principle. If the principle is rejected, Sidgwick's proof of the GHP collapses.[7]

Sidgwick, apparently confronted with a choice between maximizing the total sum of happiness and maximizing the average happiness, actually, because of his theoretical commitments,

---

(B2) "As a rational being I am bound to aim at good generally."
The "maxim of Benevolence" is:
(B3) "Each one is morally bound to regard the good of any other individual as much as his own, except insofar as he judges it to be less, when impartially viewed, or less certainly knowable or attainable by him." (382)
J. B. Schneewind, in *Sidgwick's Ethics and Victorian Moral Philosophy* (Oxford: Clarendon Press, 1977), chap. 10, offers a "negative, formalistic reading" of these three principles according to which they do not direct us to *maximize* goodness. On this interpretation, there is a problem in seeing how Sidgwick got from (B3) to the full-fledged maximizing principle that is the GHP. As Schneewind reconstructs Sidgwick's reasoning, the maximizing aspect is introduced by "the definitions of goodness and rightness": goodness by definition allows "of degrees or of comparability" and "rightness is defined in terms of bringing about the greatest good within the agent's power" (*Sidgwick's Ethics*, 307). It seems to me, however, that if "the definitions" tell us what these words mean in Sidgwick's various formulations of these principles, then it is correct to say that the maximizing element *is* present in these principles, imported by the meanings of these words. If so, then these principles can be paraphrased as they are on page 42 above.

7. John Rawls points out that the principle of average utility has a different basis from Sidgwick's GHP. See *A Theory of Justice*, §30, especially p.189. For a discussion that raises serious doubts about the plausibility of the GHP, the average principle, and attempts to combine the two principles by confronting various versions of these principles with population problems, see Derek Parfit, *Reasons and Persons* (Oxford: Clarendon Press, 1984), chaps. 16–19.

has no choice at all. The GHP directs that the *sum* be maximized, and this single ultimate principle is not to be challenged by any conflicting considerations. There aren't supposed to be any other considerations to compete with it. Although Sidgwick intuits that we are bound to produce as much good on the whole as possible, this sort of case challenges this "intuition"; no *genuine* intuition is challenged in this way. To insist upon thus maximizing the sum of utility, while dismissing the fact that each individual is apt to be less happy seems neither reasonable nor humane. It is not clear that this is a happy result from a utilitarian perspective, given the view's avowed connections with benevolence. The GHP (and one or more of the "axioms" from which it is derived) fails in this case to meet Sidgwick's own requirements for self-evidence. It fails, moreover, in the same way that maxims of the morality of common sense fail. What Sidgwick demonstrates once again is that the claim that a certain principle unfailingly in every case tells us what we should do will sooner or later encounter cases that make the claim doubtful.

IN RESPONSE to a different problem, Sidgwick was compelled to acknowledge another substantive principle, one concerned with the distribution of happiness. This principle was independent of the GHP, and the potential for conflict between the two was clear. The utilitarian method for resolving such conflicts was not available to Sidgwick in this instance, so he availed himself of the Absolutist Response. The upshot is that the resulting position is open to the sorts of objections that Sidgwick deployed against dogmatic intuitionism.

The problem arose for Sidgwick when he considered the perennial problem for utilitarians of how to choose among different distributions of the same quantity of utility. Neither the GHP nor the principle of average utility gives preference to one distribution of utility over another when the quantities involved are the same. Sidgwick's solution was as follows.

> We have to supplement the principle of seeking the greatest happiness on the whole by some principle of Just or Right distribution of this happiness. The principle which most Utilitarians have either tacitly or expressly adopted is that of pure equality — as given in Bentham's formula, "everybody to count for one, and nobody for more than one." And this principle seems the only one which does not need a special justification; for, as we saw, it must be reasonable to treat any one man in the same way as any other, if there be no reason apparent for treating him differently. [416–417]

It is strange that Sidgwick should mention "Bentham's formula" in this connection, since only a few pages later he says explicitly that this "formula" is not a principle of distribution at all.

> Bentham's dictum must be understood merely as making the conception of the ultimate end precise — laying down that one person's happiness is to be counted for as much as another's (supposed equal in degree) as an element of the general happiness — not as directly prescribing the rules of conduct by which this end will be best attained. [432]

The problem is this. It is implausible to say that it does not matter how a given quantity of happiness is distributed, but the utilitarian principle provides no grounds for preference. Thus another principle is required. Adopting another principle here, however, is a very serious step for a utilitarian. It is not sufficiently appreciated, I think, that the move Sidgwick makes here (like similar moves that other utilitarians make in similar circumstances) is profoundly at odds with the utilitarian enterprise. The principle that Sidgwick adopts at this point is that, quantity of happiness being the same, equal distributions of happiness are to be preferred to unequal ones. There

[45]

is no *utilitarian* justification for this principle. Sidgwick's justification for the principle is that unequal distributions must be justified, whereas equal ones do not require justifications.

The basis for the claim that only equal distributions do not require justification is the idea that in distributing things equally, one is treating each individual "in the same way." Sidgwick intuits the principle that "it must be reasonable to treat any one man in the same way as any other, if there be no reason apparent for treating him differently." It will follow from this principle, however, that it is reasonable to distribute happiness to individuals equally, provided that it can be shown that only by distributing things in this way would one be treating individuals "in the same way." This proviso, however, does not hold. I treat different individuals in the same way if I allocate to each a share that is proportionate to his height, or to her age, or to the value of the property he owns, or if I give each individual exactly as much as she requests. There are indefinitely many ways of determining how much of something to give to an individual, and as long as I use the same criteria impartially to determine each individual's share, I treat each in the same way. Sidgwick is simply adopting here a substantive moral principle that favors equal distributions of happiness. It is by no means an implausible principle to use—it has a certain basis in what Sidgwick calls the morality of common sense. As he introduces the principle, however, it cannot have a utilitarian basis; it is independent of the general-happiness principle.

If a utilitarian acknowledges a substantive moral principle that does not have a utilitarian basis, the utilitarian enterprise is thereby imperiled. What happens when the nonutilitarian principle conflicts with the GHP? Sidgwick's response to this question is absolutist. The nonutilitarian distribution principle can come into play only when the choice between distributions is indifferent from a utilitarian point of view, only when one has to choose between different distributions of the same quantity of utility. The two principles cannot conflict. This, however, has all the defects of the Absolutist Response to the question of how conflict problems are to be resolved. From a practical standpoint, Sidgwick's solution appears arbitrary and doubtful.

If Sidgwick is right in adopting this nonutilitarian auxiliary principle, equal distributions have some real force as considerations in practical affairs. (This consequence, of course, is incompatible with a hedonistic theory of value.) Equal distributions must be in some contexts desirable and properly have some claim to the attention of a practically reasonable individual. Consider, then, a situation in which we must choose between the following alternatives.

(1) Action α having the consequence that a certain quantity of happiness, n, is distributed very unequally.
(2) Action β having the consequence that a quantity of happiness, n', is distributed equally.

Suppose that n is slightly larger than n': On Sidgwick's view, one should choose action α because it results in a greater quantity of happiness. The equality-of-distribution consideration has no weight unless the quantities of happiness involved are equal. Is this reasonable, however, in a circumstance where the difference in the total sums of happiness produced by the two alternatives is very small, but where one distribution is equal and the other very unequal? If the distribution consideration matters—if it has weight independently of utilitarian considerations—why should it be taken into account only where the alternative courses of action distribute absolutely equal sums of utility? Why should a small difference in the total sum of happiness, a difference as small as one likes, outweigh the distribution consideration when the difference with respect to the relative equality of the distributions of utility is very great? The position of Sidgwick and the utilitarians who have followed him in this is most peculiar. They feel constrained to

[47]

admit the validity of a consideration independent of quantity of utility, an admission that runs counter to the utilitarian program. To minimize the theoretical disharmony occasioned by this admission, they declare that differences in the quantity of utility, however small, are to be given absolute precedence over the distribution consideration, no matter how uneven the distribution that maximizes utility.

This theoretical maneuver, however, is simply ad hoc. Clearly there is no way within a purely utilitarian theory to resolve conflicts between the General-Happiness Principle and an independent, nonutilitarian principle — no way to balance differences in quantity of utility against inequalities of distribution.[8] Having admitted the practical force of the latter as a consideration, however, the utilitarian has no utilitarian way of accounting for this force. Equally, however, there is no way for a utilitarian to justify the claim that the GHP *always* takes precedence over the independent distribution consideration. The theoretical vacuum through which these principles fall is complete.

Sidgwick has exhibited the implausibility of the notion that familiar maxims of morality can be made to play the role required of rules by the passive conception of rationality. The complexity of practical affairs and of the world defeats the attempt to formulate principles that in every case correctly tell us what we should do. Sidgwick's attempt to improve upon matters by adopting the single utilitarian principle is wrecked by the ineluctable plurality of the practical and by the fact that the claim that the GHP simply tells us correctly what to do is no more plausible when confronted with certain cases than the same claim made for such principles as "One should fulfill express promises and distinct understandings."

The remedy for these difficulties is not to seek more complicated or more abstract formulations of practical principles, but

8. This point is made by D. D. Raphael in "The Standard of Morals," p. 4.

rather to give up altogether the passive conception of rationality with respect to rules. Intellectual practice in the practical sphere — our own tendencies in thinking about such matters — proceeds as though there is a multiplicity of considerations whose relevance is often problematic and which often conflict with one another. If we abandon the passive conception, we give up the notion that we must discover rules that solve these problems for us. If such problems get solved, *we* do it — perhaps with the help of rules.

As long as we retain the passive conception of practical reasoning, if we suppose that all or most of our problems can be resolved by rational means, then the possible answers to the question of how relevance and conflict problems are properly resolved appear to be these: If we suppose that rules solve practical problems, then we must hold that there are numerous rules of the sort postulated by the Absolutist Response or we must hold that there is just one rule with the features described by the Utilitarian Response. If we regard the difficulties involved in both of these alternatives as intolerable, then we must give up the notion that *rules* solve relevance and conflict problems. The Intuitionist Response acknowledges that reasoning cannot be described exhaustively as doing what rules tell us, but this view still accepts the idea that properly *something* tells us what to do at every point. The Intuitionist Response says, in effect, that in telling us what to do, reason, at certain crucial points, speaks to us directly rather than through the medium of rules.

If we give up the passive conception of practical reasoning then at least one additional response can be given to the question of how relevance and conflict problems are properly resolved. This is the subject of the next chapter.

[3]

The Contextualist Response

THE TASK in this chapter is to set out an account of how relevance and conflict problems are properly resolved which is free from the difficulties of the Absolutist, Utilitarian, and Intuitionist Responses. The account will have to have the following features. (1) It will recognize the existence of a multiplicity of irreducibly different practical considerations, including moral considerations, that from time to time come into conflict with one another. (2) The account will reject the notion that practical rationality is simply a matter of doing what principles direct. What must be explained is how reasonable individuals use practical considerations, including rules, in dealing intelligently with practical problems. This use will involve active application of the considerations—interpretation and adaptation of them. (3) The account must enable us to understand how cases can be made for solutions to relevance and conflict problems, how reasons can be given in support of such solutions. It must be made clear how such cases can establish that certain solutions are better than others. The first requirement rules out the Utilitarian Response, the second the Absolutist

Response, and the third the Intuitionist Response to relevance and conflict problems.

The alternative to these three responses which I will recommend is based upon the idea that practical considerations — including the things we call moral considerations — have many different points or functions. These considerations are associated with ways of pursuing a variety of interests, fulfilling various needs, and solving many different kinds of problems that arise in our lives. Understanding the point or points of a practical consideration involves understanding and appreciating the way (or ways) with which it is associated. So, for example, we have ways of dealing with severely injured people, and a certain respect for human life is one consideration that is prominently associated with these ways. We have ways of raising children, and providing for their safety and fostering in them the power of autonomy are among the important considerations here. We have ways of dealing with people whose religious beliefs differ from our own, and religious toleration is an important consideration. We have an enormous variety of such ways (practices, procedures, activities, routines), and there are indefinitely many practical considerations. These ways and their associated considerations have been discovered and developed over time, sometimes more or less independently of one another. As the ways are employed in various situations, they must be mutually adjusted so that they can be pursued with a minimum of interference.

What I call relevance and conflict problems arise when these various ways, which have been developed to deal with specific situations that people have encountered, run into certain sorts of difficulties. When circumstances arise that are sufficiently different from those in which a certain procedure was developed, it may be unclear whether the way is applicable in the new circumstances, whether the associated considerations are relevant in the novel situation. For example, it was recently discovered that comatose individuals with certain characteris-

[51]

tics will never regain consciousness. Normally, there is a strong case for sustaining the lives of severely disabled individuals, and the consideration of respect for life is a strong element in the case. In the unprecedented case of the individual who is *known* to be *irreversibly* comatose, however, it is not clear whether the consideration of respect for life is even relevant; it is not clear whether such individuals are alive or dead. This is a relevance problem, and what is at stake here is whether it is reasonable and proper to treat such irreversibly comatose individuals as we have heretofore treated living but severely damaged individuals. (For a discussion of this problem, see Chapter 5.) Other novel circumstances may arise that juxtapose problems of living in unprecedented ways, so that the application of one way to an aspect of the problem will interfere with the use of another way with another aspect of the problem. Moral problems involving conflicting considerations typically take this form.

The foregoing characterization of moral relevance and conflict problems is extremely general and highly abstract. The generality and abstractness is necessary because of the extraordinary complexity and diversity of the phenomena being characterized. The difficulty of offering a general description of all moral relevance and conflict problems is comparable to that of offering a brief, general characterization of all technical problems, including those that arise in such diverse technical activities as musical composition, eye surgery, and corporate management. Still, though, from the perspective I advocate, one can make the following general observations about how moral relevance and conflict problems are properly resolved. The solution of such problems will involve adapting ways—which formerly have been more or less successful—to novel situations and to one another when they conflict. As these ways are altered by such adaptation, the associated considerations are themselves more or less changed. We will have succeeded in solving a relevance or conflict problem to the extent that the altered ways will enable us to deal with the sorts of matters addressed

[52]

by the old ways, while at the same time enabling us to cope with the unprecedented situation. It is important too that any disruptions elsewhere occasioned by the modifications be tolerable.

This view of how relevance and conflict problems are properly resolved emphasizes the concrete contexts in which such problems arise. The solution of such problems is to be sought in the meanings or points of the considerations involved, and the considerations derive their points from the roles they have played in the solution of past problems. The actual problem itself is to be understood as arising from an unprecedented difficulty encountered in applying tried and more or less true ways to a unique situation. The context in which the problem occurs, including its actual historical antecedents and the larger social setting in which it arises, will determine its nature, the resources for its solution, and whatever solution the problem admits of. Thus, I will call this view the Contextualist Response to the question of how moral relevance and conflict problems are properly resolved.

The Contextualist Response, then, rejects the Absolutist thesis that moral considerations are fixed from eternity in a form that is perfectly precise and consistent. On this account, the extent to which our morality is relevant to our problems and internally harmonious — that is, consistent, is an intellectual and cultural achievement. We cannot rest in whatever relevance and harmony have been achieved, because new circumstances continually arise that engender unprecedented relevance and conflict problems. Solutions to these new problems will require further adaptation and modification of our ways. What will be a satisfactory solution to such a problem will be determined by reference to what is at stake in it and how possible solutions will affect our lives, our ability to cope with further problems. On this view, we have no more reason to suppose that moral knowledge takes the form of a deductive system than we have to suppose that our knowledge of how to deal

[53]

with severe weather, broken bones, or insect pests takes such a form.

This conception of the nature of moral relevance and conflict problems and of their proper resolution is very different from the conception that lies behind the Intuitionist Response. The latter assumes that all that is necessary for a correct solution to such a problem is that a competent judger attend to the particular problem and the considerations as they are found in the problem. The judger simply ascertains which consideration is more important by scrutinizing each. The relation of the problem under scrutiny to other problems and to life in general is not thought to be relevant. The character and significance of the considerations as they occur in the particular problem is revealed directly to the competent judger, who scrutinizes these particulars in isolation from other problems and general considerations. No reasons can be or need be given for the judgment that such and such a consideration prevails. On the Contextualist Response, by contrast, it is the relationship of considerations in a particular problem to other things that determines what solution is better. General matters are involved in a solution, on the Contextualist Response, and justifications, cases, can be made for various solutions. We can often explain why in a certain problem one consideration is more important than another.

The Contextualist Response accepts the existence of many different moral considerations reflecting the complexity of human life and the variety of problems faced in living such a life. The classical utilitarian notion that all these considerations can be reduced to one for purposes of practical reasoning is rejected at the outset.

Most moral theories regard moral considerations as phenomena external to human beings, most often as rules or principles whose source and authority are problematic. It is helpful in understanding the Contextualist Response to think of moral considerations as phenomena internal to individuals — internal in the sense that the locus of these considerations is taken to be the learned dispositions of individuals. Moral considerations are items of practical knowledge which, in individuals, take the form of character traits — complex learned dispositions consisting of knowhow, skills, concerns, values, and commitments. Moral considerations such as respect for life, respect for autonomy, and religious and political toleration are internally related to ways we have developed for dealing with certain matters, but the ways themselves are best understood as the exercise or the exhibiting of certain learned dispositions. Practical considerations exist only when people have developed certain ways or practices, and these in turn exist only when people have certain learned dispositions. By reflecting upon these phenomena internal to individual men and women — these learned dispositions — we can investigate how practical considerations are properly taken account of in practical reasoning.

In order to emphasize the idea that moral considerations are located in learned dispositions and to have a shorthand way to refer to this conception, I will call this the thesis that moral considerations are character traits. If it seems odd to say that a moral consideration *is* a character trait, I ask the reader to keep in mind the above explanation.

Moral learning, like other kinds of learning, is a matter of acquiring from other people a variety of ways of doing various things, thus reaping the benefit of others' knowledge of living and coping with the world. Unless we are to remain morons, practically speaking, we must at the same time learn to adapt the ways we learn to circumstances that vary in indefinitely many ways from the circumstances in which we were taught. Being able to make such adaptations intelligently requires some understanding and appreciation of the uses or points of the ways, some knowledge of how the world works, and a sense that there are better and worse ways of doing things. On this

[55]

view, learning how to do things, learning to value things, and learning to be critical are internally related to one another. In moral reasoning concerning hard cases — cases in which considerations conflict, for example — the aim is to adapt the ways we know. To the extent that the altered ways will preserve the points of the original ways or something sufficiently like these points, with a minimum of disruption elsewhere, we will have reasoned successfully.

There exists at least one worked-out version of this view, in John Dewey's *Human Nature and Conduct*, a book to which the following account is indebted.[1] One catches glimpses of the view elsewhere. The advantages of a view that takes moral considerations to be character traits are not at present sufficiently appreciated. One advantage is this. When moral considerations are conceived externally as rules, our role with respect to them appears to be passive; we are simply to do as the rules direct. The moral rules we know, however, do not unambiguously tell us what to do in every case where we require direction, and, with disconcerting frequency, they give us conflicting directions. Some theorists hope to reformulate moral rules to give them the required degree of precision, comprehensiveness, and consistency. Such programs, however, encounter intractable difficulties. Individuals who proceed reasonably and intelligently in rule-governed activity do not simply passively do what the rules direct; they actively apply the rules. Some suppose that there are principles that tell us how to apply moral rules. This move, of course, is futile; it reintroduces the very difficulty it is intended to circumvent. The intellectual motive for the move is the fear that unless the application of rules is itself governed by rules, it will be done arbitrarily. The dilemma here is a false one. The phenomenon of adapting a practical

---

1. I am also indebted on a number of crucial points to Frederick L. Will. See his "The Rational Governance of Practice," *American Philosophical Quarterly* 18 (1981), 191–201.

skill to an unprecedented situation can provide a model for an activity that is neither passively doing what a rule directs nor arbitrary. The view that moral considerations are character traits enables us to exploit this analogy.

THE SORT of reasoning that is called for in solving moral problems belongs to the genus "practical reasoning." It is useful at the outset to remind ourselves of certain salient features of what we might call our practical educations. From infancy, we learn to do a great many things. At first we simply try to imitate what others do. Sometimes other people lead us through the steps until we learn to perform the routine on our own. Often, we do not understand why things are done as they are done until later. We simply reap the benefit of others' knowledge and experience. It is of paramount importance for us, however, to learn to adapt these routines to variations in circumstances. Mechanical, unthinking performances — rote performances — are in some situations efficient, but our environment is sufficiently complex and fluid that routines need continually to be adapted to changed circumstances if they are to continue to work. If we cannot so adapt what we learn, any sort of difficulty or barrier will simply bring everything to a halt, leaving us stymied. Of course, understanding what the routine is for and how the steps learned contribute to its purpose is necessary for us to be able to adapt the routine to novel conditions.

Practical learning is not merely a matter of storing up knowhow that we later may or may not decide to use. Our lives, consisting at the outset in random movements and instinctual activities, are deflected and channeled by the practical education we receive. These lessons mold our lives, and the activities that are learned become the form and substance of our lives. Practical education is learning how to live, and thus it involves acquiring both the ability and the propensity to do certain things. As we learn to do such things as reading and taking part in family life, we come to appreciate the point of these things and the values and standards implicit in them. What we learn has a motivational component. So far, what is acquired in practical education is similar to a set of character traits.

The marvelous plasticity of response of which human beings are capable involves the ability to adapt old routines to new circumstances. Intelligence and understanding are exhibited in such adaptation. The things that we learn to do from others are in many cases routines that have been refined and improved by countless other people who have mastered these activities, adapted them to their own circumstances and needs, and passed them on to others. Practical knowledge, like science, is cumulative and changing. Both reflect the experience and ingenuity of countless other people. The intelligent use of what we learn from others requires both an understanding and an appreciation of the achievement of others together with an ability to adapt that knowledge and a willingness to do so. There is a creative tension between the appreciation of the value of what one learns from others and a willingness to change it. One can neither "stand pat" nor divest oneself of what one has learned from others. Being critical, then, is not something brand-new that is added at a later stage of an individual's practical education; it is implicit in nearly every lesson from the start. To be critical, in an important sense of this term, is to be good at seeing how what one already knows can be changed so that it can be brought to bear upon unprecedented situations. Perfecting this ability is facilitated by becoming self-conscious about it, and this may take place in the later stages of one's education. The ability itself, however, is learned with the earliest lessons. Learning how to do something, then, will also involve learning, to some degree, how to reason practically.

[58]

THE CLAIM that "moral consideration" is a species of the genus "practical consideration" is a familiar one. There is apt to be considerable resistance, however, to the suggestion that the points made in the preceding section about practical education and practical knowledge apply as well to the moral. For one thing, if the nature and origin of moral considerations are substantially the same as those of other kinds of practical considerations, what distinguishes the moral ones from the others? It cannot be said, I think, that moral considerations share one distinctive role or fulfill one particular function in our lives. It is my contention that a proper understanding of how moral relevance and conflict problems come about and how those should be resolved requires that we appreciate that moral considerations play a variety of roles in our lives. The question of how to differentiate the moral from the rest of the practical is further complicated by the fact that there are currently many different conceptions of morality. These different conceptions are related to the fact that we are presently located at the confluence of diverse cultural and historical traditions and also to the fact that there are a number of competing philosophical conceptions of morality.

Those who assume that moral considerations are homogeneous and strikingly different from all other practical considerations might reflect upon the fact that the idea of "the moral," in its contemporary sense, is a relatively recent development. Many works from earlier periods that are central to the subject we call "moral philosophy" do not use the word 'moral' or any word accurately translated by it.[2]

---

2. According to Alasdair MacIntyre, the Greek 'ethikos', meaning "pertaining to character," was translated by the Latin 'moralis', a word invented by the Romans to translate 'ethikos'. The early uses of the English 'moral' were to translate 'moralis', although 'moral' also came to be used as a noun meaning the practical lesson taught by a story. It is not until the sixteenth and seventeenth centuries that 'moral' is taken to contrast with 'prudential', 'legal', and 'religious'. See his *After Virtue*, 2d ed. (Notre Dame: University of

Central cases of moral considerations tend, however, to have certain characteristics. There will be, in addition, peripheral instances of moral considerations that will lack certain features of central cases, but will be related in one of several ways to central cases.[3] I will try to indicate briefly some of the characteristics of moral considerations.

Within the collection of things embraced by current notions of the moral, moral considerations tend to have the following features. They contrast with practical considerations that are technical in that they tend to be relevant in a variety of different areas of life, whereas technical considerations pertain to a relatively narrow range of activity and interest. There are sorts of practical knowledge that are needed only by some people — people who, because of their circumstances, have special tasks to perform and special problems to solve; the division of labor in a community, for example, brings about such circumstances. There is, on the other hand, practical knowledge that is apt to be needed by every individual in a community in the course of his or her life. Thus the sort of technical consideration that would be taken account of in carpentry or medicine belongs to a set of considerations that pertain specifically to making things of wood or to healing. Moral considerations have a wider range of potential relevance; they pertain to living generally. Moral considerations, taken together, might be characterized as considerations consulted by one who knows how to live. Technical considerations consulted by a carpenter in woodworking are to skill at carpentry as moral considerations consulted in making decisions about the conduct of life generally are to what Aristotle set out to describe in his account of *phronesis* (practical wisdom).

Notre Dame Press, 1984), pp. 38–39. See also Anscombe, "Modern Moral Philosophy."

3. For a discussion of the distinction between central and peripheral cases and the importance of this distinction for philosophy, see Chapter 4 below.

Another feature characteristic of moral considerations is that they are connected with techniques for solving problems arising from the peculiarly social dimension of human life. Human beings are animals that live in communities, and morality pertains to problems encountered in so living. Morality, in a variety of ways, enables and fosters community; for it to fulfill these functions, it must be shared. A community's morality is a shared set of ways of providing conditions necessary for community and for solving certain problems people encounter in community living. Private moralities, of course, are possible, but these yield peripheral cases of moral considerations. Private moralities are like diaries written in private codes or talking to oneself. These are all variants — phenomena that are derived from and parasitic upon practices that are shared.

A third characteristic of moral considerations — one that distinguishes them from such things as considerations of etiquette — is their relative importance. This importance is connected with the necessity of morality for community and the extensive influence of morality on all of our ways. These three characteristics of moral considerations — their broad relevance to living generally, their connection with enabling and fostering community living, and their relative importance — are interconnected.

Moral considerations tend to be more important than matters of etiquette. (Thomas Hobbes described the latter as "small morals.") This is not to deny that a matter of etiquette might be on some occasion of enormous importance. Sometimes, small things are of great moment, as when a kingdom is lost for want of a nail. Generally, however, statecraft is more important for the welfare of kingdoms than single horseshoe nails. It is sometimes thought that by blurring the distinction between moral and other practical considerations, one depreciates moral considerations. I am claiming, however, that importance is an essential feature of morality.

A community's morality consists for the most part in certain ways of dealing with a variety of problems that its members face in living with one another. The relevant problems tend to be ones that must be solved if cooperative activity, mutuality, reciprocity, and community life are to be successful. Prominent among the problems with which morality is concerned are those arising from conflicts between individuals and those arising from conflicts between individuals' interests on the one hand and the community's interests on the other. For one thing, the community must somehow mobilize its resources and bring them to bear on a wide range of problems, including economic difficulties, natural disasters, and wars. Such mobilizations generate conflicts of interest.

A COMMUNITY'S ways of dealing with such problems develop over time — the community and its ways have a history. On this view, a community's morality embodies and reflects a people's collective wisdom such as it is. The community's ways reflect the experience of an enormous number of individuals in dealing with the problems of living together in a chaotic and often hostile world. Our community's morality is the precipitate of the practical wisdom of countless individuals, and as such it deserves our respect. On the other hand, our history reveals certain outright failures to cope as a community and also a considerable amount of muddling through. Moreover, our community's successes have been successes with past problems. New, unprecedented problems will require changes in old ways. Respect for morality must coexist with the realization that intelligent adaptation of old ways to new problems is required so that the morality can continue to deserve that respect.

If it is correct to view morality as a collection of various ways that people have developed over time for dealing with a variety of problems they face, then the point about the necessity of adapting these ways to new circumstances is important for a moral philosophy that aspires to be of use in solving difficult moral problems. One implication of this point is that neither the individual who regards morality as a set of hard-and-fast exceptionless principles nor the individual who attempts to turn his back on the morality he learned from others and live entirely by his own lights will find it easy to act intelligently in moral matters. This has obvious implications for the absolutist and utilitarian accounts of how relevance and conflict problems are properly resolved.

Some moral decisions are fairly routine; a situation is seen to be sufficiently similar to problems solved in the past that the same solution will suffice in the present case. These are the easier problems. The hard ones, of course, will be in some way unprecedented — no already worked-out way of proceeding will lie at hand. It may be unclear what considerations apply. Problems currently pressing involve such difficult questions as: For moral purposes does a living human fetus qualify as a person? Are irreversibly comatose individuals alive or dead? Both these questions arise when we ask whether the moral requirement that we protect and preserve the lives of persons is *relevant* to certain problems. Other difficult problems may involve an unprecedented conflict of considerations, as when affirmative action programs designed to promote equality of opportunity in employment conflict with seniority systems and merit systems which themselves were responses to demands for fairness and which have long been accepted as bases for reasonable expectations concerning individuals' rights with respect to their employment.

To APPRECIATE what is involved in our efforts to adapt ways of coping in order to solve moral relevance and conflict problems, it is useful to reflect on some prominent features of our *moral* education. Among the many things we learn from infancy is how to conduct ourselves toward others in a great variety of situations. This, of course, is not a single lesson, nor

[63]

is what is learned a single activity or technique. Generally, moral lessons are not sharply separated from other practical lessons. Our circumstances from the very start are social, and practically everything we learn to do involves some sort of encounter with others. Depending upon what we are doing and the situation, we encounter others as protectors, as guides, as companions, as rivals, as bystanders who nonetheless can make certain claims upon us — and so on. We learn that, in various contexts, we and others involved have roles. Certain things are expected of us. All this is a going concern before we arrive upon the scene. What we learn with respect to certain aspects of such situations substantially is our moral education. This too consists in learning how to do a great many things. In many different lessons, we learn a great many different ways of acting. To the extent that we acquire at the same time an ability to proceed with these activities in a way that is reasonable and intelligent, we will acquire an ability to modify these routines, these ways of acting, so that they will serve us in novel circumstances where the original routine as we learned it encounters difficulty. This will include situations in which two ways of proceeding — learned completely separately and independently of each — both apply, but in such a way that they conflict with each other.

Much philosophical thinking about ethics is based upon the assumption that what lies behind the morality we in fact learn from others are principles that unambiguously specify what is to be done in every circumstance in which morality is relevant. Little sophistication is required to see that the maxims we learned at parents' knees, the Ten Commandments, and the like do not specify with the desired clarity and consistency what is to be done. Some infer from this that the ethical theorist's task is to fix up these maxims, to reformulate them so that they unambiguously prescribe one and only one course of action. The reformulation may be conceived as a matter of making explicit well-known exceptions to a multiplicity of moral max-

[64]

ims, or it may take the form of reducing the number of maxims by specifying a few more general principles that are intended to prescribe unambiguously what the maxims direct only vaguely and confusedly. The difficulties to which such programs inevitably lead are described in Chapter 2 above; I will not repeat them here. Instead, I wish to raise the question, why should we assume that morality is like this at all? Why not assume instead that these maxims are verbal instructions and reminders used in inculcating and sustaining the learned ways and values, the character traits, that are the locus in us of morality? On this view, the familiar moral maxims no more comprise morality than the verbal instructions of driving teachers uttered during lessons comprise the art of driving an automobile. Note here that it is not at all plausible to suppose that behind the driving teachers' utterances is a body of precepts that prescribe unambiguously for every driving situation what we should do.

Generally, acting reasonably and intelligently in practical matters consists in more than just doing what rules say, more than just passively and blindly following the rules. The intelligent individual actively applies rules to the matter at hand. This is an intellectual activity that itself can be done well or badly, intelligently or stupidly. Central to this activity are such tasks as determining whether a certain rule applies when this is problematic and resolving conflicts when rules conflict in particular cases. It is often assumed that there are principles that unambiguously tell us how to do such things. This, of course, is futile; the assumption reintroduces the very difficulty it is designed to circumvent. The assumption is dictated, of course, by the belief that unless the activity of applying rules is itself governed by rules, it will be done arbitrarily, governed by caprice. This is a false dilemma. It is based upon the notion that the only alternative to doing exactly what one is told by a rule is to act arbitrarily. The phenomenon of adapting a practical skill to an unprecedented situation can provide

[65]

a model for an activity that is neither passively doing what a rule directs one to do nor arbitrarily doing whatever strikes one's fancy. Situations arise in which one would like to employ a familiar procedure, but one is prevented from doing so, either because the procedure one knows will not work in the situation or because using it will have unduly costly consequences. In such a situation, applying the rule or procedure *well* (that is, intelligently) might involve changing the procedure in such a way that it to some degree performs the function of the old procedure at a tolerable cost. Included in the cost, here, is the extent to which the modification disrupts other things. One who does this may also hit upon a verbal formulation—a rule in the sense of an instruction—that describes the revised procedure in a way that is an aid in remembering the revised procedure and teaching it to others. This rule, however, did not exist beforehand and did not guide one in the process of adapting the procedure. Rather, such a formulation is, like the revised procedure itself, a result or product of the process. I am not denying that things guide us in performing such intellectual tasks. I *am* denying that anything simply tells us what to do. We work it out, using things we already know.

Some of these abstract and general points about practical learning and thinking can be illustrated by considering property. How do we learn about property? We begin to learn at a very early age what belongs to whom and what difference this makes. These two things, obviously, are learned together, because there is no point in learning to classify things as hers, his, and mine, without learning at the same time what difference it makes to her, him, and me that things are so classified. Of course, the difference lies in how we feel and act toward things so classified. Learning what things belong to whom and what difference this makes is not a single lesson. We learn this in doing a great many things in everyday life that involve the acquisition, distribution, sharing, exchange, and use of things that are possessions or are candidates for that status. This is a very complicated matter. An articulated systematic understanding of why we have the complex institution of property we have, what the various rationales are for doing things in these ways, and the advantages and shortcomings of these ways is a sophisticated intellectual accomplishment. Certain individuals spend a lifetime acquiring and maintaining one of a number of kinds of expert knowledge in this area—legal, economic, historical, and so on. Most of us are not experts in one of these ways, but we do have considerable practical knowledge about such matters—some have more than others, of course, and this knowledge includes an appreciation of the importance of the institution of property.

We are continually surrounded by things that belong to someone or other, and what we feel we can and cannot do at any moment is apt to be influenced by the practical implications of the institution of property. More often than not we are unaware of this influence; we take account of property unthinkingly. When I arise in the morning, the clothes I consider wearing are all my clothes. It never occurs to me to wear a coat hanging from a neighbor's clothesline. I do not consider wearing that coat because it is someone else's. The choice of means of transportation and the routes I follow to work are similarly restricted—usually without any thought on my part—by considerations of property. So it goes throughout the day. It is no exaggeration to point out that the influence of property upon us is ubiquitous and pervasive, and to a considerable extent unnoticed by us. We have learned a complicated system of ways of behaving and have absorbed those lessons so thoroughly that we follow these ways, for the most part without thinking about them. The idea that property is something external to us in the form of a set of rules that we from time to time consult and obey does not fit very well with the facts.

Property, of course, is only one moral institution among a great many others. We could go on to consider what we have learned to do because of various social roles we occupy—family member, neighbor, friend, colleague, citizen, and others. We would find here, too, that the influences of these things upon our activities and thoughts are many, complex, pervasive, and, to a considerable extent, unnoticed by us in our daily lives. Not only are our learned ways many and various, they are continually influencing us—sometimes all at once. Not only have we learned many different and separate ways, we have learned to put them together, to adjust them to one another so that we can more or less use them simultaneously. This, however, is a never-ending struggle. The world—including other people—continually changes, requiring us to modify our ways if they are to continue to serve us. The modifications may themselves create interferences and conflicts with our other ways, requiring further readjustments. In such circumstances, we become aware of these ways, focus our attention upon them, and think about how we can readjust them in the light of our difficulties. If we proceed unthinkingly here, we invite disaster. It makes no small difference, moreover, how one thinks.

SEVERAL OF the points made in the last section are points John Dewey made by means of a technical notion of "habit." A "habit," he said, is "that kind of human activity which is influenced by prior activity and in that sense acquired; which contains within itself a certain ordering or systematization of minor elements of action; which is projective, dynamic in quality, ready for overt manifestation; and which is operative in some subdued subordinate form even when not dominating activity (40–41)."[4] Once we acquire a "habit" such as walking, according to Dewey, the "habit" influences us all the time, whether we are actually walking or not: "The habit of walking is expressed in what a man sees when he keeps still, even in

4. In this chapter, numbers in parentheses in the text refer to pages in John Dewey, *Human Nature and Conduct* (New York: Henry Holt, 1922).

dreams. The recognition of distances and directions of things from his place at rest is the obvious proof of this statement. . . . Everything that a man who has the habit of locomotion does and thinks he does and thinks differently on that account" (37–38).

All "habits," on Dewey's view, are continually operating, influencing whatever we do. That there be some considerable degree of adaptation of these operations to one another, so that they operate harmoniously, is a clear necessity. This integration of "habits," Dewey said, is "character": "Were it not for the continued operation of all habits in every act, no such thing as character could exist. There would be simply a bundle, an untied bundle at that, of isolated acts. Character is the interpenetration of habits" (38).

The interrelationship among an individual's habits, on this conception, is clearly very intricate and complex.

> Of course interpenetration is never total. It is most marked in what we call strong characters. Integration is an achievement rather than a datum. A weak, unstable, vacillating character is one in which different habits alternate with one another rather than embody one another. The strength, solidity of a habit is not its own possession but is due to reinforcement by the force of other habits which it absorbs into itself. Routine specialization always works against interpenetration. [38–39]

Learning what belongs to whom and what difference this makes would be described in Dewey's terminology as acquiring a habit or a complex of habits that must be integrated with and adjusted to other habits. (I have been using the phrase "learned way" where Dewey would use "habit.") Once acquired, not only will this "habit" influence what we do with certain objects, and so forth, that are belongings, but it will affect how we see things, how we think about things, what we take to be alternatives in deliberations where considerations of property do not explicitly arise. When I think about what to wear to

[69]

work, it does not occur to me to wear what is hanging from my neighbor's clothesline, even though those clothes are before my eyes. This obviously makes a difference in how I think on this occasion about what to wear, even though the matter of what belongs to whom does not come up in my thoughts.

The upshot of our practical education, including its moral aspect, is that we acquire certain habits of action — including habits of thought. Many of these habits are the loci in individuals of the ways of the community, developed over time, of solving problems of living together. By acquiring similar habits, individuals are able to share a way of life. Community is thus possible. In other words, we acquire values, learn to appreciate things, learn to live with one another. The problem of effecting the "interpenetration of habits" in individuals is, to a considerable extent, the localized version of the problem of making a community's ways harmonious and mutually reinforcing.

Learned ways — habits — influence us continually. Typically, however, we become aware of these ways as moral considerations when the circumstances are such that old lessons need to be modified before they can be applied or where some of the moral considerations that have a claim upon us come into conflict with one another or with something else. On such occasions, practical reasoning is called upon to perform its function. The task to be performed in practical reasoning and the sort of difficulty that calls upon these intellectual skills are conceived very differently on the pragmatist's view from the way the task and its difficulty are conceived on other views.

There are any number of plausible things one might say about what we do in practical reasoning. For example:

(1) We attempt to reach decisions in accordance with the canons of (practical) rationality.

(2) We strive to discover the best course of action, all things considered.

[70]

These two dicta are true, but they are about as informative about the character of practical reasoning as the dictum that scientists seek the truth is about what science is. These innocent truisms, moreover, when combined with certain other ideas, reinforce certain misconceptions about practical reasoning. So, practical reasoning described as "activity in accordance with the canons of rationality" suggests someone passively following very explicit instructions — like a neophyte cook working with a cookbook in one hand. The idea of seeking the best possible solution is transmuted into the notion of producing as much good as possible, so that all practical problems are thought to be like the problems of a minister of agriculture charged with maximizing grain production. Classical utilitarianism provides a misleading description of the general nature of practical problems — of what it is in such problems that causes us difficulty and challenges our knowledge and ingenuity. It also misdescribes the nature of the good we aim at when we seek the best solution to a particular practical problem. Of course, we want a solution that is satisfactory, one we can be happy with, but this does not mean that our *problem* is to maximize happiness or satisfactions.

Dewey described "deliberation" in this way.

> The office of deliberation is not to supply an inducement to act by figuring out where the most advantage is to be procured. It is to resolve entanglements in existing activity, restore continuity, recover harmony, utilize loose impulse and redirect habit. . . . Deliberation has its beginning in troubled activity and its conclusion in choice of a course of action which straightens it out. It no more resembles the casting-up of accounts of profit and loss, pleasures and pains, than an actor engaged in a drama resembles a clerk recording debit and credit items in his ledger. [199]

On the utilitarian view, the good we aim at in practical reasoning is thought of as one homogeneous thing; one justifies

[71]

various acts and policies, on this view, by showing that each produces more of this one homogeneous thing than alternative acts and policies. On the pragmatist view, practical reasoning, whether about individuals' actions or community policies, attempts to solve specific concrete problems; the good aimed at is a complex of intricately related things whose structure is dictated by a set of circumstances that limits possibilities, a context that includes a world and a way of life. One remark of Dewey's sums up a view of the good aimed at in deliberation that contrasts strikingly with the utilitarian conception: "In quality, the good is never twice alike. It never copies itself. It is new every morning, fresh every evening. It is unique in its every presentation. For it marks the resolution of a distinctive complication of competing habits and impulses which can never repeat itself" (211).

If the claims I have made about practical considerations are true, then the difference between these two accounts of practical reasoning and its proper aim is of great importance. The practical knowledge that constitutes our resource for solving practical problems is divided among and embodied in a great many different practical considerations. Each consideration involves knowhow, skills, appreciations, and values acquired from past experience — the experience of oneself and others — with quite a specific sort of problem. The knowledge embodied in the consideration is in that sense relatively specialized. When problems arise involving conflicts of considerations or uncertainty about the relevance of a consideration, it is the relatively specialized practical knowledge that needs to be called up and pressed into service, if we can find ways to adjust it in order to make it serve. The utilitarian account directs our attention away from the loci of the very practical knowledge that is our resource for solving practical problems. It would have us consider something so abstract that we are diverted both from the real problem and from the tools we have for dealing with it. A conflict between loyalty to a friend and loyalty to one's country is a problem involving friendship and citizenship. The problem is to discover how, in one particular case, one can be, insofar as possible, true to both. To approach the problem as a problem about maximizing satisfactions represents it in an unhelpful and misleading way.

AN IMPORTANT advantage of a contextualist or pragmatist view of morality and practical reasoning is that it can provide a useful response to the problem of how relevance and conflict problems are properly resolved, a response that is free from the intractable difficulties of the Absolutist, Utilitarian, and Intuitionist Responses. There are objections to pragmatist views, however, that lead some to dismiss them without a hearing. Certain of Dewey's remarks positively invite such objections. For example:

> For practical purposes morals mean customs, folkways, established collective habits. This is a commonplace of the anthropologist, though the moral theorist generally suffers from an illusion that his own place and day is, or ought to be, an exception. But always and everywhere customs supply the standards for personal activities. They are the pattern into which individual activity must weave itself. [75]

This provokes the following sort of response: People whose lives are dominated by custom, who take custom to be the ultimate authority in practical affairs, are primitive and unenlightened. Their way of life contrasts sharply with that of individuals who take rationality to be the guide of life. If it were true that morality is simply custom, then morality would be a stupid guide. Morality, however, is related to reasonable, enlightened conduct. It is a mistake, then, to identify morality with custom.

Dewey's response to such an objection is that it equates customs with unenlightened customs, whereas some customs are intelligent and reasonable, while others are not (77–79). There are people who take certain customs as authoritative because, as they might say, "We have always done things this way." There are people who lack the imagination to see alternatives to old ways and to ask if any would be an improvement. It is possible, on the other hand, for people to take a "custom" (a shared way of doing things) as authoritative because they see good reason to have some custom and see that the particular custom they have well suits their purposes.

In a theater program, for example, there is the instruction, "In case of fire, walk, do not run, to the nearest exit." This reminds us of a "custom." We see a need for some "custom," because if everyone bolts for the exit in a fire, the results are ghastly. The "custom" might be to remain in one's seat and sing "Nearer My God to Thee." The actual "custom" is obviously better, more intelligent than this imagined alternative.

In using the terms 'habit' and 'custom' as he does, Dewey exacerbates certain misgivings about his view. We are accustomed to contrasting habitual behavior with reflective action. We use the word 'habitual' to refer to certain sorts of actions done unthinkingly. Even here we should note that the routine operations one performs today without thinking about them may have been in the past worked out with great care, intelligence, and ingenuity. Dewey, however, does not restrict the use of the term 'habit' to tendencies to act unthinkingly. He uses the term 'custom', moreover, for "established collective habits" so that 'custom' too embraces a variety of ways of doing things, including some of great complexity and ingenuity.

Dewey claims that morality is a certain kind of custom, and it is objected that morality must be different from custom. Morality consists in standards by which conduct is to be evaluated; it is an ideal, a standard of how things ought to be. It cannot be merely custom, which is nothing more than regularities in how people in fact act. No mere custom could be the sort of standard that morality is.

Dewey's view, of course, is that any standard of right and wrong, including moral standards, emerges from human life and activity. Some patterns of behavior that are well adapted to our needs and purposes must exist before we notice the difference between those that are well adapted and those that are not. Only then is it possible for us to form the "habit" of cultivating the well-adapted ones — only then can we appreciate the possibility of rationality as a guide to life. A plausible reconstruction of the development of such standards is this: To begin with, people learned ways of doing things. Some genius (or series of geniuses) got the glimmer of the idea that sometimes things went better and sometimes things went worse and undertook something like proto-reflection on this idea. There emerged something like the idea that if one proceeds in a certain way, things are apt to go better (a hunt will be successful, infants are more apt to live, a wound is less likely to become infected). Such nuggets of information were gleaned, applied, and taught. Proto-standards were born — people came to have a sense of better and worse (right and wrong) ways of doing things. This is a necessary first step in becoming critical, in becoming rational. Seeking and cultivating better ways of doing things can itself be cultivated as a "habit" — it can be applied, refined, taught to others. The potential sophistication and complexity of such a "habit" is limitless.

Standards, developed in this way, are not mere by-products of the evolution of practical knowledge. They are implicit in it; as they develop they become powerful forces for further development.

> Language grew out of unintelligent babblings, instinctive motions called gestures, and the pressure of circumstance. But nevertheless language once called into existence is language and operates as language. It operates not to perpetuate the forces which produced it but to modify and redirect them. It has such transcendent importance that pains are taken with its use. Litera-

[75]

tures are produced, and then a vast apparatus of grammar, rhetoric, dictionaries, literary criticism, reviews, essays, a derived literature *ad lib*. Education, schooling, becomes a necessity; literacy an end. In short, language when it is produced meets old needs and opens new possibilities. It creates demands which take effect, and the effect is not confined to speech and literature, but extends to the common life in communication, counsel and instruction. [79–80]

Every institution — "family life, property, legal forms, churches and schools, academies of art and science" — developed its own standards, which became then "additional forces" that spur further development. "They open new avenues of endeavor and impose new labors. In short they are civilization, culture, morality" (80). Such standards are reflected in our habits — they form our lives. To the question of how standards, developed in this way, have any authority, Dewey responds that these things are implicit in the activities that comprise our lives. We cannot escape them. "The choice is not between a moral authority outside custom and one within it. It is between adopting more or less intelligent and significant customs" (81).

CONSIDERATIONS that we would classify as moral, then, are many. They are learned in many different contexts, and they serve a variety of purposes. Their influence pervades our lives, forms our lives. We are aware of these influences, however, as moral considerations only intermittently. Often, we become aware of moral considerations only when they conflict with some plan of ours. These circumstances help sustain the illusion that our plans, our interests, our hearts' desires and ambitions form one area of concern and morality a more or less separate area. Moral considerations can seem external intrusions upon our desires and interests, which makes them in another way seem external to us. This misconception encourages moral theorists to attempt to show on "purely nonmoral"

[76]

grounds that certain moral principles are reasonable. Another sort of philosophical view insists upon the "autonomy" of moral considerations — their importance and value, it is claimed, is intrinsic and in no way derives from their relationship to other things in our lives. These contrary positions share the assumption that one's view of one's life — one's "life-plan" — is sufficiently independent of all moral considerations to enable one to form a clear conception of one's interests and plans with all moral elements abstracted from them. In fact, though, the central elements in people's life-plans are such things as engaging in commerce or politics or scientific research, marriage, child-rearing, and pursuing friendships. Such activities and goals exist only within the network of moral considerations. There can be corrupt scientific researchers — individuals who are willing to fake data and results in order to make reputations for themselves and enjoy the accompaniments of success. Their aims and activities, however, are different from those of genuine scientists; they are parasitic upon the goals and practices of the scientific community, and their activities subvert that enterprise. These activities and the network of other practical matters, including the moral, interpenetrate. It is an illusion to suppose that we can separate them.

The following passage from a novel by Evelyn Waugh about London's "bright young people" at the outbreak of World War II illustrates the absurdity of attempting such a separation.

> There was a young man of military age in the studio; he was due to be called up in the near future. "I don't know what to do about it," he said. "Of course, I could always plead conscientious objections, but I haven't got a conscience. It would be a denial of everything we've stood for if I said I had a conscience."
>
> "No, Tom," they said to comfort him. "We know you haven't a conscience."

[77]

"But then," said the perplexed young man, "if I haven't got a conscience, why in God's name should I mind so much saying that I have?"[5]

OUR CONDITION is so complex that situations often arise in which moral considerations conflict; certain aspects of a situation indicate to us one course of action and other aspects a contrary course. An important function of practical intelligence is to enable us to cope with such conflicts. Practical wisdom — being good at deciding what to do in matters pertaining to the general conduct of one's life — involves the ability in such situations to determine which considerations are really relevant and which of the conflicting considerations are more important. It involves the ability, in other words, to give the considerations the weight they should have.

On the view I am advocating, the weight that a certain consideration should be given in a particular circumstance is not necessarily given or determined by preexisting rules or principles. This point is connected with certain remarks Aristotle made in explaining his general conception of an *arete ethike* (an excellence of character).[6] Aristotle's general conception can be explained in this way: certain matters that are common in practical problems are especially troublesome for people — for example, dangers, the satisfaction of appetites, things involving physical discomfort, and matters concerning wealth and honors. People are particularly apt to make mistakes in determining the weight to give considerations when such matters are involved. Certain people, moreover, are apt consistently to make the same sort of mistake. Thus, some individuals tend over and over to give too much weight to considerations of

5. Evelyn Waugh, *Put Out More Flags* (Boston: Little, Brown, 1942), p. 47.

6. These remarks are found primarily in *Nicomachean Ethics*, Book II, chap. 6.

avoiding danger in their choices. Others, however, are able consistently to give considerations involving danger neither too much nor too little weight in such situations. They give such considerations the weight they should have — neither too much nor too little. People who choose in this way and act on their choices have the excellence of courage. Courage, then, is a sort of "mean."[7]

If asked what determines the right amount of weight to give the consideration involving danger in a particular situation, Aristotle would respond that this is determined by a *logos*, the *logos* by which a practically wise man (*phronimos*) would determine it. English translators of Aristotle render '*logos*' here as 'rational principle', which suggests to us that Aristotle thought that a *phronimos* has a general rule that tells him in every circumstance how much weight to give considerations involving danger in making choices. Nowhere, however, does Aristotle tell us what such a general rule would look like. The explanation of this, I think, is that Aristotle was not thinking that some rule tells us how much weight to give considerations involving danger in any situation. In fact, he seems implicitly to deny the existence of any such principle when he compares the determination of the mean with respect to a certain sort of consideration — that is, the determination of what constitutes giving the consideration neither too much nor too little weight, but just the weight it should be given — to the determination of the right amount of certain food in one's diet. What is neither too much nor too little but just the right amount of a certain food varies from person to person, Aristotle says. He might have said too that for the same person, it may vary from time to time, depending upon whether one is well or ill, whether one is trying to lose weight or train for an athletic contest, and so on.

7. See J. O. Urmson, "Aristotle's Doctrine of the Mean," *American Philosophical Quarterly* 10 (1973), 223–230.

The *logos* that determines the amount of a certain kind of food that I should eat—the amount that will be neither too much nor too little—is a certain sort of reasoned view of my situation with respect to this question. This reasoned view will involve an appreciation of what is at stake for me in the question of my diet and an understanding of the effects and consequences of various courses of action. The *logos* that will determine how much of a certain food I should eat will involve such things as general facts about nutrition, information about the state of my health, an appreciation of what I am trying to do and why (gain strength and/or lose weight and/or avoid a disease to which I am predisposed, and/or . . .), together with information about what foods are available, my taste in foods, the kind of life I lead (sedentary or active, stressful or serene), the dietary restrictions of my religion, and any number of other things, depending upon the situation. Some particular concatenation of goods and evils will be involved in this particular practical problem. The *orthos* (or correct) *logos* here—the view of the situation that establishes that I should eat *X* amount of a certain food—might explain how a certain diet will enable me to obtain or preserve certain important goods at a reasonable cost, while avoiding certain evils. I say the *orthos logos might* do this, because we cannot take for granted that every practical problem will admit of such a happy solution. One can only look for such a solution and hope.

When I am faced with the problem of how much of a certain food I should eat, I cannot take it for granted that there already exists a formula that will tell me the answer. I will probably have to work out the matter for myself, taking into account a unique set of circumstances. There are obviously better and worse solutions to my problem. In the course of solving my problem, I work out a rationale for a certain solution—a *logos*, an account of the matter that justifies my solution in the light of all the circumstances and considerations. This is practical reasoning.

[80]

Similarly, what determines how much weight I should give the prospect of physical danger to myself in a particular situation is a view of that situation that takes into account a unique complex of goods and evils. That view or *logos* is something that needs to be worked out by practical reasoning. Understanding Aristotle's *logos* in this way, we can say that Aristotle's general definition of moral virtue has the consequence that a courageous individual is one who consistently chooses in a way that indicates that he gives dangers to himself neither more nor less practical weight than they should have. What determines in a particular case how much weight a certain danger should have is a certain reasoned view of the situation — the view that would be taken up by someone good at practical reasoning.

If this view of practical reasoning is superimposed upon Aristotle's general definition of moral virtue, the practically wise individual is not conceived as someone who possesses a set of principles that simply say what weight to give certain problematic considerations in every situation. This is just as well, since it is implausible to suppose that anyone might have such a set of principles and impossible to explain how anyone could know that a particular set of complicated practical principles are correct in the desired way. It is tempting to say that by translating *logos* as 'rational principle', Aristotle's translators force an absolutist construction upon the text, but I am not sure that this should be blamed entirely upon the translators. Aristotle did not have one view about practical reasoning, though I am unable to decide whether he had more than one view or less.

THERE IS, however, the persuasive argument, sketched at the end of Chapter 1, for the view that if reasoned solutions to complicated practical problems are possible, there must exist general principles that prescribe these solutions and justify them. If a reason or argument can be produced to make a case for

[81]

one solution to a practical problem involving multiple considerations, such a reason or argument will necessarily involve an appeal to one or more general principles that prescribe the solution. Unless one subscribes to the intuitionist view of how conflicts among considerations are to be resolved, it appears that the possibility of justified solutions presupposes the existence of and the possibility of knowledge of general principles that prescribe these solutions. If such principles exist and can be known, then it seems plausible to regard a practically wise individual as someone who has access to these principles.

My criticism of this argument is that although the rationale that justifies a solution to a particular problem will necessarily involve reference to general considerations — principles, if you like — it does not follow that these principles must guide the solving of the problem or even that the principles must exist in the form in which they occur in the rationale *before* the problem is solved. With hard practical problems, it is often the case that the justification of a solution is itself the *product* of the practical reasoning. The *logos* and the principles it contains, in other words, rather than existing ahead of time and dictating the solution, may actually be produced along with the solution by the problem-solver.

How can such a justification that is produced along with the solution it is supposed to justify escape being ad hoc? Recall the earlier observation that practical intelligence involves a balance between an appreciation of existing practical knowledge and a willingness to adapt that knowledge to new problems and circumstances — to change it. In problems where some feature of the situation is unprecedented, so that it is unclear whether a certain consideration is relevant, it would be ad hoc simply to stipulate that the consideration is or is not relevant. If, however, we consider why the consideration in question has been a consideration in the past (what its point is), and why people have been concerned with this sort of thing, such inquiries and reflections *may* enable us to see that the concerns that have made this a consideration in other cases either are or are not involved in the present case. Such results could provide grounds for holding that the consideration whose relevance is in question should or should not be taken to be relevant in this sort of case. Where such a case can be made, one way or the other, the principle or consideration is thereby modified, and in that sense, the consideration that justifies the decision is produced along with the decision. If the practical reasoning has proceeded properly, however, the modification will be justified by reference to, among other things, the point (or points) of the consideration in question — by reference to the uses of the consideration in the past, the problems it has solved, the values it protects, the meaning these matters have for us. Practical wisdom involves, among other things, an appreciation of the points of moral considerations, an understanding of their importance that influences choices.

MORALITY IS to be viewed, I suggest, as a complicated, interrelated set of shared, learned ways. Participation in these ways requires the exercise of complexes of psychological tendencies, skills, and valuings. These complexes are character traits that exist in us. These traits are the locus in us of moral considerations, and the ways that exhibit them have points or uses or functions that we understand more or less well. The point or points of a way or a consideration will be found in our past experience. We should expect to find that these ways have enabled us to do certain important things, have contributed to the solution of certain problems, or have enabled us to prevent certain problems from arising.

David Hume described property and promising as conventions, consisting in people's commitment to certain ways of behaving, the entire system serving their needs and interests in specified ways in a particular set of circumstances. So, for example, he said about "the origin of property":

[83]

When men, from their early education in society, have become sensible of the infinite advantages that result from it, . . . and when they have observed, that the principal disturbance in society arises from those goods, which we call external, and from their looseness and easy transition from one person to another; they must seek for a remedy. . . . This can be done after no other manner, than by a convention entered into by all the members of society to bestow stability on the possession of these external goods, and leave everyone in the peaceable enjoyment of what he may acquire by his fortune and industry.[8]

In the second *Enquiry*, Hume said:

The rules of equity or justice depend entirely on the particular state and condition in which men are placed, and owe their origin and existence to that utility, which results to the public from their strict and regular observance. Reverse, in any considerable circumstance, the condition of men: Produce extreme abundance or extreme necessity: Implant in the human breast perfect moderation and humanity, or perfect rapaciousness and malice: By rendering justice totally *useless*, you thereby totally destroy its essence, and suspend its obligation upon mankind.

The common situation of society is a medium amidst all these extremes. We are naturally partial to ourselves, and to our friends; but are capable of learning the advantage resulting from a more equitable conduct. Few enjoyments are given us from the open and liberal hand of nature; but by art, labour, and industry, we can extract them in great abundance. Hence the ideas of property become necessary in all civil society: Hence justice derives its usefulness to the public.[9]

The "usefulness" or "utility" of the institution of property, according to Hume, is to forestall conflicts between people over

8. David Hume, *A Treatise of Human Nature* (Oxford: Clarendon Press, 1978), Book III, Part II, sec. II, p. 489.

9. *An Enquiry Concerning the Principles of Morals* (Oxford: Clarendon Press, 1975), sec. III, Part I, p. 188.

"external goods," thus promoting peace in society and a sense of security in the possession of these goods. This complex convention, by promoting peace and security, provides a circumstance in which people are motivated to produce external goods, thus increasing society's supply of such things. The same circumstance facilitates commerce and trade — practices that enhance the possibilities of people's satisfying their desires for external goods. Hume was not using the term 'utility' here in the sense that Bentham later gave it. Hume was thinking of various social institutions and practices as *artifacts* — as tools created by people to serve quite specific purposes. There is nothing in this idea that necessarily makes it "utilitarian" in the technical sense of that term — or "consequentialist" either, for that matter.

In this account, Hume was describing, in a general way, the point of property, of ownership as a practical consideration. As far as it goes, Hume's description is an example of an account of what property means to us. In accepting Hume's account, one is not committed to the view that any actual practices are beyond criticism, nor is one committed to any particular political position. One is committed thereby to recognizing the fact that an institution of property has certain important functions. One would do well, then, to take this fact into account in considering how a particular institution might be modified.

Some people dislike the whole idea of property. Rousseau, for example, offered a pungent account of the dark side of this institution in the *Discourse on the Origin of Inequality*. One common complaint is that the practices internal to this institution do not always have the result that commodities are distributed where they are needed. This is an important issue; one of the points of community is to foster the welfare of its members. A community that is indifferent to the plight of members who are hungry, ill, or homeless is a poor community indeed. There is no question that communities should try to ensure that their members' needs are fulfilled. The real issue is how to do this;

[85]

fulfilling such needs is not a community's only concern. We need practices that fulfill the important functions of property *and* we need ways to ensure that people's basic needs are met.[10] Actual circumstances will limit what we can do to address both these concerns effectively; among the circumstances is the fact that we have many other concerns too. A community's concerns and the ways by which it addresses them are all deeply interconnected—in Dewey's phrase, they "interpenetrate." When a way requires modification, reason requires that we consider how possible modifications affect other concerns, other ways. This is easy to say, but often difficult to do.

Such a view of practical considerations enables us to understand how one might proceed reasonably in situations where one's stock of ways of proceeding is simply not adequate as it stands to deal with a concrete problem. The aim must be to modify one or more considerations so that it applies, so that its original point is to some degree preserved, and so that one can live with the way so modified. One type of difficult moral problem involves conflicting considerations—situations in which one relevant consideration indicates one course of action and another indicates a contrary course. We might seek in such a case to modify one conflicting consideration or both so that we can act in such a way that the claims of both are satisfied. If this is not feasible, we might try to ascertain whether one consideration is more involved in the problem—whether its point is somehow more at stake than the other's. Such determinations are often difficult, but the task is facilitated by an understanding, and appreciation, of the importance in our lives of these considerations generally, together with an accurate perception of the involvement of these considerations in the particular problem at hand.

This account of moral reasoning is a very general and com-

10. For a discussion of these matters, see Michael Walzer, *Spheres of Justice* (New York: Basic Books, 1983), chaps. 3 and 4.

pressed sketch of something that often is extraordinarily complex. Examples are desirable. Actual moral problems involving conflicting considerations tend to be themselves very complicated. When we discuss real problems, moreover, it is difficult to focus attention upon the formal, the methodological aspects of the matter. The issues themselves, naturally, tend to absorb us. Problems that concern civil disobedience nonetheless provide some clear examples of problems involving conflicting considerations. Since the issues involved are familiar and well explored, such a problem can serve as an illustration.

Consider the problem faced by a civil rights leader in Alabama in 1963. This individual, who is committed to democracy and the rule of law, contemplates publicly violating laws that impose indignities upon black citizens. The aim of such violations would be to draw attention to these indignities and to dramatize the case for repeal of the laws. Various legal protests have proved ineffective, and no other means of opposing the laws is available. The conflict in such a case may be acute. To anyone who understands and appreciates the practice of democracy and the ideal of rule of law, the following points will be quite clear: If the law in question is duly enacted in a democracy and supported by a majority, then the position that one has no duty to obey such a law if one believes it unjust will be difficult to reconcile with a commitment to the ideals of rule of law and democracy. That individuals may decide for themselves what laws to obey is incompatible with the ideal of rule of law, and that individuals decide on a case-by-case basis whether to accept the decision of the majority once it has spoken is incompatible with democracy. At stake for us in these matters are such things as our freedom from the arbitrary rule of the stronger—what Rousseau called "civil liberty"[11]—and our political equality, our equality under impartial law. Reflec-

11. Jean-Jacques Rousseau, *The Social Contract,* Books I and II.

[87]

tion upon what is at stake here will make it difficult for us to feel easy about intentionally violating the law.[12] What we are reflecting upon are the points of democracy and the rule of law — the meaning, the value these things have for us. Their points are not simple things to be grasped in a moment and characterized by a phrase such as "quantum of utility." The points of the rule of law and democracy, referred to by such phrases as "civil liberty" and "equality under the law," can be understood and appreciated only if one understands and appreciates political practices that have developed in response to certain social and political circumstances. A deeper understanding of these matters would require mastery of a long and complex history. An account of the relevant political practices and associated values could be developed and illustrated by historical examples.[13] Alternatively, one might attempt a very abstract "reconstruction" of these developments in order to capture in briefer compass the meaning of democracy and the rule of law. Locke and Rousseau made such attempts, in significantly different ways.[14]

The civil rights leader, of course, was opposing unjust laws in a community that espoused democracy and the rule of law. The laws in question deprived individuals of their political rights for no good reason and dishonored those individuals undeservedly.[15] These unjust laws were incompatible with the

12. In his famous essay, Henry D. Thoreau is astonishingly insensitive to these considerations. See Thoreau's "Civil Disobedience," in Hugo Adam Bedau, ed., *Civil Disobedience: Theory and Practice* (New York: Pegasus, 1969), pp. 27–48.

13. Examples of the kind of account I have in mind abound in Walzer, *Spheres of Justice.*

14. See John Locke, *The Second Treatise of Government* and Rousseau, *The Social Contract.*

15. The wrongness of racial discrimination is not an issue here. There are no defenses of racial prejudice and racial discrimination as such that are worthy of consideration; when these matters are argued with any care, they rely on false claims. With racial discrimination as with violent crime the

[88]

community's political morality, yet they were supported by a majority of the members of the community. The complaints of the victims of these injustices were well founded, and their predicament was poignant. Laws that undeservedly dishonor members of a community are repugnant; they tend to undermine respect for law and cause discord. One is inclined to protest vigorously when one is the victim of such injustice, and one feels an obligation to help others when they are victims. When one considers what is at stake here, it is apparent that one cannot abandon the values involved in any of these considerations.

In a circumstance in which the only effective way to oppose injustice is to violate the law, the conflict is acute. The conflicting considerations have strong claims upon us, and the claims are supported by cogent reasons that survive critical scrutiny. Our aim in such a case should be to satisfy *all* such claims, insofar as we can. There is no guarantee, however, that this will be possible — that we can discover a way of giving each consideration its due. Failure will have a high cost, however. Part of the cost will be a degree of anarchy, suffering, and/or injustice with which we will have to live, in which we must acquiesce, to which we will inevitably harden ourselves. It is not an exaggeration to say that the kind of people we are and the sort of world we live in are substantially affected by how we deal with such a problem.

What would a course of action that satisfied the claims of all conflicting considerations be in such a case? Finding one seems impossible. One must either violate the law or acquiesce in injustice. John Dewey remarked that the aim in deliberation should be to devise an action "in which all [competing tendencies] are fulfilled, not indeed in their original form, but in a 'sublimated fashion,' that is, in a way which modifies the orig-

---

problem is not to show that it is wrong but rather to determine what to do about it. This is really many problems.

inal direction of each by reducing it to a component along with others in an action of transformed quality" (194). With this idea in mind, consider the following statements by Martin Luther King, Jr., made in defense of a policy of civil disobedience in opposition to segration laws.

> In no sense do I advocate evading or defying the law as the rabid segregationist would do. This would lead to anarchy. One who breaks an unjust law must do it *openly, lovingly.* . . , and with a willingness to accept the penalty. I submit that an individual who breaks a law that conscience tells him is unjust, and willingly accepts the penalty by staying in jail to arouse the conscience of the community over its injustice, is in reality expressing the very highest respect for law.[16]

John Rawls makes a similar point.

> [Civil disobedience] expresses disobedience to the law within the limits of fidelity to law, although it is at the outer edge thereof. The law is broken, but fidelity to law is expressed by the public and nonviolent nature of the act, by the willingness to accept the legal consequences of one's conduct. This fidelity to law helps to establish to the majority that the act is indeed politically conscientious and sincere, and that it is intended to address the public's sense of justice.[17]

These points apply to a particular case in which an individual aims to change an unjust law by publicly disobeying it. The individual has hit upon a course of action that is an obvious attempt to oppose injustice. One cannot overlook the fact that it is an action of intentional disobedience of the law, but the individual at the same time affirms a commitment to an ordered society under the rule of law by ensuring that the

16. Martin Luther King, Jr., "Letter from Birmingham City Jail" in Bedau, *Civil Disobedience,* pp. 78–79.
17. Rawls, *A Theory of Justice,* pp. 366–367.

action is nonviolent and by a willingness to accept the legal penalties. This is by no means a facile expression of fidelity to law; it is not a cheap gesture. Thus, the tendency to obey the law gets expressed in a "sublimated fashion" even as a man or woman purposely disobeys the law.

Whether this can be regarded as a satisfactory solution to a particular conflict problem may depend upon many things. The idea that a sincere respect for law can be expressed in an act of purposely breaking the law can be made plausible. On the other hand, experience has shown that when conscientious people engage in such principled disobedience of the law, others are encouraged to engage in unprincipled disobedience. Civil disobedience is a socially risky undertaking, because it puts a strain on the general effectiveness of the rule of law in a community. Of course, unjust laws also tend to undermine respect for law. In some circumstances, civil disobedience is a serious candidate for the status of a reasonable solution to a certain kind of difficult problem involving conflicting considerations.

To the extent that civil disobedience is a novel solution for us to such a conflict problem, adopting such a solution will require us to change our understanding of the ideal of rule of law, of respect for law as a moral consideration. The conception of this ideal that recognizes civil disobedience as a justifiable course in the proper circumstances is different from the conception that does not. The former conception has the advantage that it can be harmonized in certain circumstances with a commitment to oppose injustice, whereas the latter conception of the rule of law cannot. Whether in practice this advantage outweighs the disadvantages of such an ideal is a question I will not pursue any further.

This discussion of civil disobedience is intended as an illustration of how a moral conflict problem is properly resolved according to the Contextualist Response. It is meant to clarify the view and to show that the actual moral deliberations of

[91]

serious people do take this form. According to this view, the moral considerations that conflict in a particular situation are associated with ways that we have developed for certain purposes. In this example, because of a particular configuration of circumstances, respect for law and commitment to democracy dictate one course of action, and a sense of justice dictates a contrary course of action. The Contextualist Response counsels an attempt to modify the considerations and the ways so that the meanings, the points, of the original considerations are preserved as far as possible with a minimum of disruption elsewhere. This general advice seems compatible with a great many courses of action, but in a concrete example of a difficult conflict problem, the nature of the particular considerations and the actual circumstances of the problem impose strict limitations upon what can be done that is consistent with the Contextualist Response. If the idea of civil disobedience were unfamiliar, it would be very difficult to see any way of acting that would be responsive to the claims of all relevant considerations. The civilly disobedient course of action is admirably ingenious, and this very ingeniousness is a source of difficulty. The conception is so sophisticated that many people do not understand it. The notion that one can sincerely express respect for law in an act of intentional violation of it is subtle and complex — too much so for some. This, of course, is one reason why civil disobedience is risky. The explanations offered by King and Rawls, however, can be understood as efforts to convince us that conceptions of democracy and the rule of law that recognize civil disobedience as legitimate in certain specified circumstances are consistent with our understanding of the meaning, the points, of the political practices that are associated with these considerations. A case is being made for an amended — and more complex — version of these considerations and practices.

The Contextualist Response, then, is based upon the notion that moral considerations are irreducibly multiple; the view

[92]

directly addresses the problem of how to deal with such multiplicity in view of the endless potential for conflict. This response provides an account of how we as rational agents, with the practical knowledge, interests, and values that we have, actively use practical considerations to deal with our problems. There is no suggestion in the view that anything simply tells us what to do. It is clear, moreover, that on this view cases can be made in defense of various solutions to conflict problems — there are clearly better and worse solutions. The Contextualist Response, then, is free of the crippling difficulties that afflict the Utilitarian, the Absolutist, and the Intuitionist Responses.

SOME PHILOSOPHERS will complain that what I am offering here is common sense and not philosophy. Philosophy is supposed to provide *theories*. The Contextualist Response, as I have presented it, simply asserts that we have a vast stock of practical knowledge gleaned from our experience with many kinds of past problems. When we encounter new problems, we must somehow adapt items from the unsystematic body of lore as best we can. We are aided in such tasks by our understanding and appreciation of what these items of knowledge have meant to us in the past. At the outset, I promised to describe how moral relevance and conflict problems are properly resolved. Does the Contextualist Response, as I have described it, provide us with *a way* of resolving such problems? It does not provide us with "a decision-procedure," an algorithm, for solving such problems, so it does not provide "a theory" in that sense. This is not, however, a fault in the Contextualist Response. On this view, the challenging conflict and relevance problems that we encounter in the practical sphere are precisely those for which no already worked-out method of solution exists. The Contextualist Response, appropriately, stresses the importance of intelligent, calculated improvisation and the virtue of resourceful inventiveness in adapting our practical

[93]

knowledge to unprecedented difficulties. It provides answers for the question of how solutions to such problems might be justified, how something might be shown to be a better or worse solution to such a problem. The tendency to suppose that this is shallow philosophy at best, that profound philosophy would offer a "decision-procedure" here, has its roots in the passive conception of practical reasoning. The assumption is that profound practical philosophy will tell us what to do. I will not repeat the criticisms of the passive conception, but a characteristically blunt passage by Dewey is relevant:

> The more complicated the situation, and the less we really know about it, the more insistent is the orthodox type of moral theory upon the prior existence of some fixed and universal principle or law which is to be directly applied and followed. Ready-made rules available at a moment's notice for settling any kind of moral difficulty and resolving every species of moral doubt have been the chief object of the ambition of moralists. In the much less complicated and less changing matters of bodily health such pretensions are known as quackery. But in morals a hankering for certainty, born of timidity and nourished by love of authoritative prestige, has led to the idea that absence of immutably fixed and universally applicable ready-made principles is equivalent to moral chaos. [238]

THE CONSIDERATIONS that are involved in moral and other practical problems have their origin in the way we live, in the ways we have devised or learned from others for coping with practical matters. This is the source of the authority of these considerations over us as rational beings, and it is the source of our commitment to them. These traits or tendencies were developed in actual concrete circumstances, where they served us more or less well. Nothing guarantees that they will continue to serve us or that they will not clash head-on in circumstances posing novel problems. It is the work of practical reason to adapt them, to make them operate effectively and harmoniously when the need arises. It cannot be taken for granted that this task always will be or even can be performed successfully. Consistency of principles, values, and practices is in fact a result that is never finally and permanently achieved. In the practical sphere, as in the scientific, answers and solutions, however ingenious and admirable, invariably lead to further questions and problems.

George Eliot saw more deeply into these matters than did her utilitarian friends.

> No formulas for thinking will save us mortals from mistake in our imperfect apprehension of the matter to be thought about. And since the unemotional intellect may carry us into a mathematical dreamland where nothing is but what is not, perhaps an emotional intellect may have absorbed into its passionate vision of possibilities some truth of what will be — the more comprehensive massive life feeding theory with new material, as the sensibility of an artist seizes combinations which science explains and justifies. At any rate, presumptions to the contrary are not to be trusted. We must be patient with the inevitable makeshift of our human thinking, whether in its sum total or in the separate minds that have made the sum.[18]

18. George Eliot, *Daniel Deronda,* chap. 41.

[4]

The Importance
of Importance

In developing an account of morality that is contextualist and pragmatic (in the philosophical sense), I have described morality as a heterogeneous collection of shared ways of solving problems of living together, ways developed by individuals in real-life situations and modified by countless other individuals in order to adjust the ways to one another and to changing circumstances. I have stressed the complexity and pervasiveness of the body of ways that structure our lives. Dewey's technical notion of "habit" is useful here, because it reminds us that we are continually influenced by the ways in which we were schooled, whether we are aware of those influences or not. It may in particular instances require considerable effort and reflection to appreciate the ramifications of various moral considerations. Moral considerations are on this view similar in nature to other practical considerations, differing mainly in their greater importance. Moral reasoning is conceived as a process for adapting these ways and harmonizing them as unprecedented circumstances disrupt their smooth operation. This view also indicates how it is that we may learn more about the functions of our moral practices, deepen our understanding of them, by reflecting upon what is implicit in our practical educations, by noting how well or badly these ways enable us to get on, and by studying history in order to understand how these ways developed.

One thing that recommends this view of morality and practical reasoning is the account it affords of how relevance and conflict problems are properly resolved. To determine the relevance of certain considerations and their proper weight in actual moral problems, one must understand the points of the considerations. The point(s) of a consideration will lie in the function, the use of the practice that the consideration embodies. The idea that an understanding of the points of moral considerations is indispensable for solving moral problems is plausible because we would not expect to be able intelligently to apply or to resolve conflicts between *any* rules or procedures whose uses and points we do not understand. The task with particular moral problems, on this view, is to determine the applicability of moral considerations and to resolve conflicts among considerations in ways that can be defended by showing that (1) the solution proposed retains, insofar as possible, the necessary functions of the old ways, (2) the solution addresses the needs of the present situation, and (3) the modifications of our ways implicit in the solution are ones we can live with. In order to develop such solutions, we need to understand the points of the considerations involved, the uses of the ways, and the value of the things at stake.

It will be objected that this account so far is at best only a part of a philosophical account of practical reasoning. The account simply takes it for granted that there are practical considerations that are crucially related to certain important values. The sorts of problems that moral practices are supposed to be ways of solving are presumably situations in which certain goods are in jeopardy or in which certain evils threaten. The account does not explain either the source of these values or how their status as values is to be ascertained. Rationality, the objection continues, requires more than the determination of relevance of considerations and the resolution of conflicts among considerations. Each of the considerations must be tested critically. Its *point* — the value(s) that it is designed to secure or protect — must be shown to be genuine; that is, some philosophical basis must be provided for the belief that certain values deserve to be taken into account by reasonable individuals.

Much of the basis for a response to this challenge will be found in the account already given. The values that give our ways their point and function do not, in general, exist separately from and independently of those ways themselves. Our values and the activities that comprise our lives, including the activities intended to secure and preserve these values, are related internally to one another. The critical assessment of values, which is an important part of practical reasoning, cannot be undertaken in isolation from the activities that comprise our lives and the relationships of these things. One could not have even a rudimentary understanding of a human activity or institution without some understanding of the norms of better or worse that apply to the activity and without an understanding of the interest(s) the activity serves. Practical education and education in values occur simultaneously; they are the same lessons.

The main idea is ancient. Aristotle made the point that for some kinds of things, what makes something a thing of that kind is what it does. An eye *sees*, a teacher *teaches*, a human being *lives a certain sort of life* (a different form of life from those of horses, worms, and geraniums). The sort of activity or function that makes a thing a thing of kind K, Aristotle calls the *ergon*, the "work," of a K. Thus, teaching is the *ergon* of a teacher, and so on. This is an important notion for a philosophical account of value, because if things of kind K have an *ergon*, a good K is a K that does its *ergon* well.

[98]

'A so-and-so' and 'a good so-and-so' have a function [*ergon*] which
is the same in kind, e.g. a lyre-player and a good lyre-player,
and so on without qualification in all cases, eminence in respect
of goodness being added to the name of the function (for the
function of a lyre-player is to play the lyre, and that of a good
lyre-player is to do so well). . . . [*NE*, 1098a 8–12][1]

Where does the standard for judging whether the *ergon* of a
K is done well or poorly come from? Aristotle said: "For a
flute-player, a sculptor, or any artist, and in general, for all
things that have a function or activity, the good and the 'well'
is thought to reside in the function." [*NE*, 1097b 25–28].

Standards by which human activities are done well or poorly
"reside in" the activities in the sense that in order to have an
idea of a specific activity, one must have *some* understanding of
what it is to do the activity well or badly. Someone who ham-
mers on the keys of a piano is not *playing the piano*. To be able
to distinguish between playing and random noise-making—an
ability necessary in order to qualify for possessing the most
rudimentary idea of piano-playing—one must have some conception of what is proficiency at piano-playing—of what constitutes being *good enough* at the activity that what someone does
qualifies as piano-playing. Someone's effort at piano-playing
may be so bad, so inept, that it does not qualify as piano-
playing.[2] This rudimentary understanding of what piano-playing
is requires some rudimentary grasp of what music is, what
interests are served by music, some understanding of the place
of music in human life. The idea of piano-playing encapsu-
lates a notion of what interests piano-playing serves and some
basis for judging whether the activity is performed well enough
so that in a general way those interests might actually be served

1. The translation of the *Nicomachean Ethics* is that of W. D. Ross in Ross,
ed., *The Works of Aristotle Translated into English*, vol. 9 (Oxford: Clarendon
Press, 1915).
2. I recall, years ago, someone's making a similar point with this very
example. I regret that I cannot remember whose example this was.

by it. Of course, a more sophisticated understanding of piano-playing will involve more complex standards for judging whether the playing is done well or badly and a more sophisticated understanding of what music is all about. Standards by which piano-playing is judged are internal to this activity, "reside in" this activity, in the sense that any understanding of what piano-playing is requires at least some understanding of what constitutes performing the activity well enough for it to count as an instance of piano-playing.

Such is the generality of the presence of norms and standards "in" activities, practices, and institutions, that the "ideal" of a value-free account of human activity and society is simply impossible. These matters cannot be understood apart from values, apart from standards and the interests that give these standards their rationale. This point is made forcefully by John Finnis in his discussion of "descriptive jurisprudence."[3] Finnis argues that an adequate account of the nature of the institutions of human law must acknowledge the centrality of certain ethical norms in these institutions. These institutions are, Finnis maintains, indispensable for securing certain fundamental human goods, for satisfying certain "requirements of practical reasonableness." That these goods should be secured, that these requirements should be satisfied, are matters prescribed by moral principles.

Finnis's argument, in outline, is this: The object of descriptive jurisprudence is to give an adequate account of the nature of human law. To do justice to the complexity of the subject matter of such an inquiry, a theorist must identify "central cases" of law and legal institutions. This complexity is connected with the variety and complexity of the actual things that are called 'law' in one sense or another. Once the proper "central cases" are identified, then the various things that are

---

3. *Natural Law and Natural Rights*, chap. 1. Numbers in parentheses in the text in discussions of Finnis's views refer to pages of this book.

denominated 'law' and 'legal institutions' can be seen as instances of central cases or as variants of them, related in various ways to central cases. It is crucial that the "central cases" be properly identified and characterized. This can be done only by a theorist who understands what it is about those institutions that is *important* and *significant*. In the absence of such an understanding, the facts about what things are called 'law', 'legal institutions', and so on, will be a jumble. The theorist must grasp, according to Finnis, "the practical viewpoint that brings the law into being as a significantly differentiated type of social order and maintains it as such" (14). Certain social institutions exist because they serve a "moral ideal," Finnis says, "a compelling demand of justice" (14). These institutions are the central cases of human law. In this way, Finnis argues, an understanding of practical reasonableness and the moral law that secures the basic aspects of genuine human flourishing is necessary for jurisprudence.

The project of providing a useful descriptive account of the law which is "value-free," Finnis argues, is infeasible. The argument is readily generalizable to any human institution, as Finnis says. The implications of this point for the "ideal" of a value-free social science are obvious. The point is adaptable to a variety of things other than institutions, moreover, including some fundamental biological notions.[4]

Consider the position of the theorist who surveys the subject matter of descriptive jurisprudence. To describe these data, one must decide what counts as law for the purposes of the description. In real life, legal practices and institutions are not clearly differentiated from other social institutions. Actual legal institutions, moreover, at various times and in various places differ from one another in a great many ways. Thus there are

---

4. For a discussion of norms in biology, see my *Virtues and Vices* (Ithaca: Cornell University Press, 1978), chap. 1.

many odd borderline cases of legal institutions — in certain primitive cultures, for example, or in Uganda under Idi Amin.

The idea that what the theorist must do is discover what all and only those things called 'law' have in common (the Platonic program) does not get us very far. The subject matter resists this treatment. More plausible, in view of the actual subject matter, is the hypothesis that the various things called law have no features in common. Rather, they resemble one another in a number of overlapping ways, some sharing one feature, others sharing another similarity — much as members of a single human family may resemble one another (the Wittgensteinian program).

But although the family-resemblance hypothesis fits the subject matter better than the Platonic thesis does, it provides no understanding of the unity of the subject matter called law. It points to the fact that things called law resemble one another in various ways, but we also know that these same things will resemble a great many other things that are not called law. How are we to understand the grouping of *certain* similar things under the rubric of law and the exclusion of other things?

Following Aristotle, Finnis proposes to organize the subject by seeking central or primary cases and arranging other cases in relation to the central ones as variant or deviant cases. In discussing friendship, Aristotle said:

> There must, then, be three kinds of love, not all being so named for one thing or as species of one genus, nor yet having the same name quite by mere accident. For all the senses of love are related to one which is the primary, just as is the case with the word 'medical', and just as we speak of a medical soul, body, instrument or act, but properly the name belongs to that primarily so called.[5]

5. *Eudemian Ethics*, 1236a 17–20. The translation is that of J. Solomon in Ross, ed., *The Works of Aristotle Translated into English*, vol. 9.

To identify central cases of a kind, Finnis says, one must understand what is significant and important about the kind of thing
being studied. I understand this to mean that one must know
how such things as law are important to people generally, what
needs and interests law serves—one must understand the roles
played by law in human life.

Tools and artifacts provide relatively simple examples for
illustrating central and peripheral cases of a kind. One dic-
tionary says a knife is "a cutting instrument with one or more
sharp edged blades, often pointed, set in a handle." This definition must be understood as applying to central cases of knives;
otherwise, it is open to obvious counterexamples: pallet knives,
toy knives, ceremonial daggers, broken knives, dull knives, par-
tially made knives, and so forth. Understanding the definition
as embracing central cases of knives, however, we can then
proceed to see such things as dummy knives and defective
knives as variants related in specifiable ways to the central
cases. In a community with such cutting instruments there
will be defective knives because of imperfect manufacture or
damage. Children will play at knife-wielding, and there is reason to see that they do not use real knives for play. These are
clearly peripheral or secondary instances of knives in the sense
that they exist because the primary instances exist to serve the
interests and needs knives serve. There would be no damaged
or unfinished knives unless there were (or had been) finished,
undamaged knives. Finnis extends this point to more complex
and abstract artifacts.

> By exploiting the systematic multi-significance of one's theoret-
> ical terms (without losing sight of the 'principle or rationale' of
> this multi-significance), one can differentiate the mature from
> the undeveloped in human affairs, the sophisticated from the
> primitive, the flourishing from the corrupt, the fine specimen
> from the deviant case, the 'straightforwardly', 'simply speaking'
> (*simpliciter*), and 'without qualification' from the 'in a sense', 'in
> a manner of speaking', and 'in a way' (*secundum quid*)—but all

[103]

without ignoring or banishing to another discipline the unde-
veloped, primitive, corrupt, deviant or other 'qualified sense' or
'extended sense' instances of the subject matter. [10–11]

Someone who understands what law is, then, will have an
understanding of what the role of law is in human affairs. This
provides the basis for an understanding of when a particular
human institution performs this function well or badly. One
who knows what law is has some grasp of the standards by
which legal systems are judged to be good or bad. This provides a basis for discriminating central cases of legal systems
from those that are primitive, defective, corrupt, and so forth.
Finnis maintains—plausibly, I think—that a central function
of a legal system is to fulfill certain moral requirements, certain "demands of justice." A major barrier to the appreciation
of this important claim is removed by the following point: The
existence of corrupt or primitive legal systems, such as that
under the Nazis or Idi Amin, does not refute the claim that
law is essentially an instrument for fulfilling certain moral
requirements, certain demands of justice, any more than the
existence of eyes in blind individuals or fetuses refutes the dictum that the eye is the organ of sight.

VALUES ARE essential components of activities, practices,
and institutions. An understanding of what an activity is will
require an understanding of standards by which performances
of the activity are judged to be done well or badly, and this
will require an understanding of the needs and interests that
the activity serves. What I have called practical education necessarily involves education in values, including moral values.
To the extent that the education is truly practical, it will involve
coming to appreciate certain values.

A critic of such pragmatic conceptions of morality and practical reasoning might concede this point about the internality

of values to activities, practices, and institutions, and still maintain that the account of the justification of values is seriously incomplete. The final assessment — the critic will point out — that pronounces a certain value worthy to be secured and protected cannot in *every* case rest upon the claim that the goods in question derive their value from *other* things, because this will only raise the question of the certification of these other putative values. This cannot go on ad infinitum, for if our certification of *any* particular value presupposes our having certified something else, we are not going to be able to certify the value of anything. What appears to be required in a complete account of practical reasoning — which has not yet been provided — is an explanation of how some value can be certified as genuine without an appeal to other values already certified. In other words, what is thought to be lacking is an account of how *basic* values are justified, so that we can understand how to begin the process of justification of value.

The central point in this objection is a familiar one. Here is Aristotle's version of the same argument with 'desiring' and 'choosing' substituted for 'valuing'.

> If, then, there is some end of the things we do, which we desire for its own sake (everything else being desired for the sake of this), and if we do not choose everything for the sake of something else (for at that rate the process would go on to infinity, so that our desire would be empty and vain), clearly this must be the good and the chief good. [*NE*, 1094a 17–21]

David Hume made a similar point in commenting upon an imaginary conversation.

> Ask a man *why he uses exercise*; he will answer, *because he desires to keep his health*. If you then enquire, *why he desires health*, he will readily reply, *because sickness is painful*. If you push your enquiries farther, and desire a reason *why he hates pain*, it is impossible he can ever give any. This is an ultimate end, and is never

referred to any other object. Perhaps to your second question, *why he desires health*, he may also reply, that *it is necessary for the exercise of his calling*. If you ask, *why he is anxious on that head*, he will answer, *because he desires to get money*. If you demand *Why? It is the instrument of pleasure*, says he. And beyond this it is an absurdity to ask for a reason. It is impossible there can be a progress *in infinitum* and that one thing can always be a reason why another is desired. Something must be desirable on its own account, and because of its immediate accord or agreement with human sentiment and affection.[6]

Aristotle maintained that practical wisdom — the general ability to make right decisions concerning the conduct of one's life — consists in more than being able to figure out how to get what one wants. Among other things, according to Aristotle, the practically wise man wants the right things. As he and Hume argued, there must be something "desirable on its own account." How, though, is it to be established that something is desirable on its own account?

We parallel Hume's thoughts on this question by considering the following sorts of example. If I want to walk in the woods because such a walk is pleasant or to touch a certain surface because I am curious about how it will feel, there is no need to ask what my reasons are for wanting a pleasant walk or for wanting to satisfy my curiosity about how something will feel. These things may not lead to anything else I want, yet it is appropriate to call them desirable — desirable for their own sake. There is nothing wrong with this conclusion; what, though, is its significance for understanding practical reasoning? One is tempted to suppose that we have reached bedrock in the critical assessment of value in these examples, that these cases are important paradigms of properly concluded critical evalu-

6. *An Enquiry Concerning the Principles of Morals*, Appendix I, in L. A. Selby-Bigge, ed., *Hume's Enquiries*, 2d ed. (Oxford: Clarendon Press, 1902), p. 293.

ations of considerations in practical matters. Of course, this tendency is reinforced by the line of reasoning in the passages of Aristotle and Hume just quoted. It is important to notice, though, that it is not usual to find assessments that correspond to these supposed paradigms in actual critical reasoning. If one examines a selection of actual critical discussions and deliberations of challenging concrete practical problems, it is apparent that attempts to establish things as desirable for their own sake do not loom large in such discussions. Hume's imaginary conversation in the passage quoted above is an improbable specimen of deliberation.

Proponents of the view that the genuineness of a value can be established only by connecting it with something desirable in itself may nonetheless recognize that it is not common in actual deliberations to trace considerations to the basic intrinsic goods that underlie them. This is consistent with their view, they might suggest, because in actual deliberations, the genuineness of every relevant consideration and value is not in question. People take it for granted that certain things are desirable for their own sake; the depths of justification are probed only by the philosophically minded.

This response is not satisfactory, however. In truly difficult and vexed practical questions, one would not expect reasonable people who are genuinely puzzled or who are in direct disagreement with one another to proceed upon the assumption that they are in agreement about the genuineness of the values involved. If the view about the importance of things desirable in themselves for the certification of value were correct, then one would expect to find it reflected in the intellectual practice of reasonable individuals. The fact that when thoughtful, critical people defend their views on some important political or social issue, they are not apt to focus upon the question of what things are desirable for their own sake needs to be accounted for. It is not plausible to suggest that people do not focus upon this question simply because the question is esoteric. More plausible is the hypothesis that the question of what things are desirable for their own sake does not have the importance for practical reasoning attributed to it by Aristotle, Hume, and many others.

The philosophical difficulties, moreover, in explaining how it is to be properly established that something is desirable for its own sake when something controversial depends upon its being so established, are intractable. One might say, as Aristotle does, that the things correctly desired for their own sake are things that are good in themselves, and that such things are desired for their own sake by the good man — the man possessing the virtues. This, however, does not take Aristotle very far. In his ethics, moral virtue is defined by reference to the determinations a practically wise man would make. When the account of practical wisdom, as (roughly) wanting the things a good man would want and being able to figure out how to get such things, is placed beside the account of moral virtue as (roughly) the disposition to choose in certain circumstances as a practically wise individual (*phronimos*) would think one should, it is apparent that the two accounts are circular. After traveling around the circle, one is no wiser about how the *phronimos* properly establishes in a particular case what is good in itself. Aristotle's analogy is apt: "We should not know what sort of medicines to apply to our body if someone were to say 'all those which the medical art prescribed, and which agree with the practice of one who possesses the art' " (*NE*, 1138b 30–32).

Within the matrix of assumptions made by Aristotle, Hume, and others, where the certification of every value depends upon properly establishing that something is good in itself, the project of explaining how things are properly established to be good in themselves is fraught with difficulties. Even if these difficulties could be overcome, however, the result would be an unsatisfactory account of practical reasoning. If practical reasoning is construed as a matter of choosing certain actions on the basis of their conduciveness to certain goals, and if we hold that

[108]

these goals are good independently of their relationship to anything else, we will find it difficult to explain why these goals are important and how their importance relative to one another is established. In fact, what generally matters in practical reasoning is not whether certain things are desirable in themselves, but rather how important these things are. When one must choose between fundamental goods, a rational choice will be based upon some well-founded assessment of the relative importance of the values in conflict, and the information that these are things desirable in themselves does not contribute to this assessment. In fact, it tends to make it appear that such assessments cannot be made — one must simply choose as one might choose between chocolate and strawberry ice cream. A view that does not provide an account of how such an assessment properly is made will lead in the end to noncognitivism or to a feeble intuitionism.

John Finnis sets out clearly an account of practical reasoning that has the features of the sort of view I am criticizing. Finnis identifies certain things as "basic human goods" — knowledge, life, play, aesthetic experience, practical reasonableness, friendship or sociability, and religion. The knowledge that these things are good, he claims, is self-evident and underived. Knowledge, Finnis says, "is really a good, an aspect of authentic human flourishing, and . . . the principle which expresses its value formulates a real (intelligent) reason for action" (64). "The good of knowledge," he says, "is self-evident, obvious. It cannot be demonstrated, but equally it needs no demonstration" (64–65). Finnis says at the outset that he is talking about "speculative knowledge" — knowledge sought for its own sake as opposed to knowledge "sought only instrumentally, i.e. as useful in the pursuit of some other objective such as survival, power [etc.]" (59). We do, in fact, inquire out of curiosity, the pure desire to know for its own sake, Finnis points out. Reflection upon these points, according to Finnis, leads to the realization that knowledge generally is intrinsically a good thing, though, of course, that knowledge is intrinsically good does not *follow from* the fact that we desire it.

Finnis's account of knowledge as a basic value and a fundamental aspect of human flourishing is unsatisfactory. He is surely right in the claims he makes for the value and importance of knowledge. He has, however, put himself in a position in which he cannot explain why knowledge is such an important human good.

To see this, suppose someone were to make the following claims. Scratching itches is good for its own sake. This is not deduced from the fact that we have a natural inclination to scratch itches. Anyone with a reasonable amount of experience will see that one is better off with one's itches scratched than without. This is not so just because having one's itches scratched is conducive to a good disposition, composure, and the ability to concentrate on other things. Scratching itches is good for its own sake — intrinsically good. Scratching itches is an important fundamental aspect of human good.

These claims about scratching itches are every bit as plausible as what Finnis says about knowledge, except that it is not plausible to claim of scratching itches that it is an important basic element of human flourishing. On the other hand, it is manifestly plausible to make such a statement about knowledge. The reason knowledge is important to and fundamental in human life is, I think, as follows. Any form of life that is properly described as human is impossible without knowledge. It is, therefore, not merely an element in human flourishing — good human life — but it is necessary for that form of life. The pursuit of or participation in sociability, practical reasonableness, religion, play, and aesthetic experience — some of the other things that Finnis lists as basic human goods — would be impossible without some structured set of beliefs about the world that meet certain requirements of epistemic adequacy — without, in other words, knowledge. To "participate in" such goods as Finnis lists, one needs a community with shared beliefs about the world and with a common language. Community, shared beliefs, and a common language go together; each is required for the others. It is not the fact that knowledge is desirable for its own sake that makes it *an important and fundamental* human good. Knowledge is desirable for its own sake in the sense that there would sometimes be reason to acquire it even if nothing else desirable resulted from acquiring it. Scratching itches is, as far as I can see, desirable for its own sake in the same sense, but this does not qualify it as a basic aspect of human flourishing. Knowledge is an important and fundamental good because it interlocks with, it sustains, it advances a great variety of other things that form the content of a human life. No such claim can be made for scratching itches.

Two individuals might study economics, one because he is interested in such matters (that is, out of curiosity about the subject) and another because she wants to make a killing by investing in soybean futures. Clearly their motivation is different, but the *knowledge* they seek may be exactly the same. There are not two kinds of knowledge being sought here, one desirable for its own sake and the other not. One might say that these two individuals value the knowledge differently — one intrinsically and the other instrumentally. I do not wish to quarrel with this. If one wants to know why such knowledge is generally good to have, however, the right sort of answer will have to do with the connection of such knowledge with other things. This connection is what gives such knowledge its importance. This explanation does not leave out or overlook the economics that is studied by those curious about such matters. They might be studying economics because they are curious about it, period. If, however, they wish to explain why a knowledge of economics is more important and more valuable in general than (say) an intimate knowledge of the private lives of one's neighbors — one might be equally curious about such matters — the right answer is that economics is an important subject because of its place in human life generally. This would explain why a sensible person, equally curious about economics and his neighbors, would think economics a study worthy of life-long pursuit, a worthy career, whereas the study of one's neighbors to satisfy one's nosy curiosity is not. For purposes of practical reasoning, it is the importance of a value that is generally crucial — and this is different from the question of whether the value is desirable for its own sake.

Someone who finds economic theory intrinsically interesting, however, appreciates the value of such knowledge more fully than someone who is interested in such knowledge only as a means of making money for herself. This appears to be at odds with the point that the importance of a value is determined by its relations to other things, but it is really perfectly consistent. Economic theory *is* intrinsically interesting, and someone who does not find it so is missing something. Consider, though, *why* it is intrinsically interesting. It is interesting because it illuminates an extremely important dimension of human social behavior, because it is an application of certain sorts of theorizing to such social phenomena, because it can exemplify certain qualities that are excellences in theories (elegance, simplicity, and explanatory power, for example), and, no doubt, for other reasons too. Someone who values knowing economic theory *only* instrumentally — say as an instrument for making money for herself — is narrowly focused upon only one relationship between this knowledge and the world to the exclusion of *other* existing relationships that are more central to economic theory itself and are more important in the scheme of things. So it is that someone who values such knowledge only instrumentally — that is, only because of one peripheral consequence that its possession can have — has a relatively shallow appreciation of the value of economic theory.

What would it be like for someone to value economic theory independently of its relationships to anything else? If this were understood to mean that someone took an interest in economics, ignoring its relationships to such things as commerce, psychology, and theorizing, then it is doubtful that we can imagine such a thing. Perhaps we can imagine someone's taking an interest in a particular theory as a sort of abstract pattern (but how do we describe the elements of the pattern — sounds, marks on paper, words, sentences, . . . ?). Such an interest, if it can be imagined, would be most eccentric, and it is the furthest thing imaginable from a deep appreciation of the value of economic theory. One who values knowledge of economic theory *only* as a means to making lucrative investments fails to appreciate fully the value of such knowledge in much the same way as would someone who is interested in such theories only as abstract patterns. Both are only partial appreciations that fail to grasp fully the interest and importance of economic theory. Economic theory is obviously internally related to the world of production and trade and to the practice of theorizing. One who values such knowledge "intrinsically" rather than only "instrumentally" — as these terms are normally understood — appreciates the importance of all these internal relationships. Someone who values these theories only instrumentally, on the other hand, is concerned with this knowledge only insofar as it is a means to something else (making money, for example) and is thus concerned only with one relationship of economics to other things.

Of course, one who values something only instrumentally values the thing only because it is a means to something else valued. The difference, however, between someone who, with reason, values something intrinsically and someone who values the same thing only instrumentally can be explained as the difference between a more complete and a less complete, a partial, appreciation of the thing's value. It is not necessary to hold that the thing has value independently of anything whatsoever in order to explain how it can properly be valued intrinsically. The philosophical notion that important basic goods have their value "in themselves" — independently of their relations to other things — is implausible if one considers the example

[113]

of knowledge.[7] The cost of adopting that notion as a general thesis about the source of all value is exorbitant; it is catastrophic for the theory of practical reasoning, because by severing goods from their relations with other things, we make it impossible to explain what makes these goods important.

In the following passage, an acute contemporary philosopher, influenced by Aristotle's assumptions about practical reasoning, candidly describes how matters appear from this perspective.

> In the first place the wise man knows the means to certain good ends; and secondly he knows how much particular ends are worth. Wisdom in its first part is relatively easy to understand. . . .

> The second part of wisdom, which has to do with values, is much harder to describe, because here we meet ideas which are curiously elusive, such as the thought that some pursuits are more worthwhile than others, and some matters trivial and some important in human life. . . . But I have never seen, or been able to think out, a true account of this matter, and I believe that a complete account of wisdom, and of certain other virtues and vices must wait until this gap has been filled.[8]

Because the thesis that important basic goods must have their value in themselves is widely held, unsatisfactory theoretical alternatives tend to occupy the field. Positing a single

---

7. G. E. Moore said that something is intrinsically good just in case it would be a good thing for it to exist "even if there were absolutely nothing else in the universe besides" (*Ethics* [London: Oxford University Press, 1912], pp. 100–101). How could there be a universe in which there exists a knowledge of economics and absolutely nothing else? The things that are candidates for the role of intrinsic goods, things desirable in themselves, including Finnis's basic goods, could not even exist in isolation in the manner Moore proposes.

8. Philippa Foot, *Virtues and Vices* (Berkeley: University of California Press, 1978), pp. 5–6.

Intrinsic[9] (i.e. good-in-itself) good such as pleasure becomes tempting, because this seems simultaneously to solve several problems. That pleasure is a good thing seems to need no explanation. If it is the *only* Intrinsic good, there is no need to explain why it is more important than other goods. Conflict problems, it is hoped, will dissolve before the method of the hedonistic calculus.

The hedonistic theory of value, notoriously, produces implausible results. Why, though, is it outrageous to say that quantity of pleasure being equal, pushpin is as good as poetry? Hilary Putnam examines this question and concludes:

> We *have* a reason for preferring poetry to pushpin, and that reason lies in the felt experience of great poetry, and of the after effects of great poetry — the enlargement of the imagination and the sensibility through the enlargement of our repertoire of images and metaphors, and the integration of poetic images and metaphors with mundane perceptions and attitudes that takes place when a poem has lived in us for a number of years. These experiences too are *prima facie* good — and not just good, but ennobling, to use an old fashioned word.[10]

Note that Putnam's sensible and plausible explanation of the value of poetry connects poetry with other things; it shows the place of poetry in human life generally. Simple games such as pushpin have no such relations. Poetry is a celebration of lan-

9. The first letter of 'Intrinsic' is capitalized to indicate that the term is used in the technical philosophical sense — where 'Intrinsic good' means something having value independently of its relations to anything else. There are things that have intrinsic value in the sense 'intrinsic' has when it is contrasted with 'instrumental'. There are things we find intrinsically good in the sense that we sometimes choose them even when nothing *else* desirable results from our choosing them. It is important to distinguish these senses of 'intrinsic' from its technical sense. Confusing these senses gives the claim that certain things are Intrinsic goods a plausibility it does not deserve.

10. Hilary Putnam, *Reason, Truth, and History* (Cambridge: Cambridge University Press, 1981), p. 155.

guage, and as such, it has a significance no simple game could possibly have. Consider the following passage by George Eliot.

> These familiar flowers, these well-remembered bird notes, this sky with its fitful brightness, these furrowed and grassy fields, each with a sort of personality given to it by the capricious hedge, such things as these are the mother tongue of our imagination, the language that is laden with all the subtle inextricable associations the fleeting hours of our childhood left behind them. Our delight in the sunshine on the deep-bladed grass today might be no more than the faint perception of wearied souls, if it were not for the sunshine and grass of far-off years, which still live in us and transform our perception into love.[11]

Not only are the perceptions of field, sky, and birds imbued with rich cognitive and emotional meanings by our long association with them, but, to reverse Eliot's metaphor, so too is our language. Language is, in a way, the medium in which human life takes place. Because we live with and in language, it becomes loaded with all the meanings of human experience. Poets exploit the richness of the meanings and associations with which language is laden. That John Stuart Mill in his despondency turned to poetry rather than pushpin is not to be explained *merely* as an instance of a preference shared by people of a certain sort. Of course, it is to the point to note that Mill was not an idiot, but idiots are not just individuals with eccentric tastes in their enjoyments. The atomistic conception of value I am criticizing is as deleterious for the philosophy of art as it is for ethics.

IF A proponent of Finnis's conception of practical reasoning could be convinced that knowledge is important and valuable because of its connections with other things, he might

11. George Eliot, *The Mill on the Floss*, Book I, chap. 5. This passage is quoted by John Dewey in *Art as Experience* (New York: Putnam, 1934), p. 18n.

respond that this shows that knowledge is not to be numbered among the basic goods that are properly desired for their own sake. We need to look for the basic Intrinsic goods among the things with which knowledge is connected, from which it derives its value. We have learned from Aristotle, the response continues, that eventually we must come to some thing or things that are good in themselves, things that do not derive their value from anything else but from which all other things derive their value.

Compelling as this model is, it is a bad fit with the facts. The value and importance of human knowledge derives from — that is, is explained by — its enabling, supporting, sustaining, advancing, and intensifying other things in human life. Following Finnis, we might mention among these other things aesthetic experience, play, sociability (friendship), practical reasonableness (including morality), and religion. It is the *relations* of knowledge to these other things that make major fields of inquiry and study interesting and worth devoting a life to. If, however, we are asked to explain the value and importance of these *other* things — play, aesthetic experience, sociability, and so on — it will be their relationships to one another and to other things in our lives generally that we will appeal to.

Doesn't this in the end, though, come to the same thing as saying that living a certain sort of life is Intrinsically good in the sense that it is good in itself, independently of any relations to things outside itself, and that other things derive their value from the Intrinsic goodness of that sort of life? My disagreement with Finnis begins to look like a disagreement about what the basic Intrinsic goods are — he lists several, and I am holding out for a single composite good. Must I not in the end make the claim that the goodness of a certain form of life is Intrinsic, underived, and self-evident? I want to resist this position. It is appealing only because it is dictated by the view that any sound piece of practical reasoning must have as a terminus something that is Intrinsically good. This view, however,

[117]

does not accord with the actual practice of reasoning and leads to insoluble philosophical problems. It is a barrier to one's understanding of practical reasoning.

I concur with the claim that knowledge is an important basic element of human good, of human flourishing. Its value and importance in general, however, are to be explained by its central place in human life, particularly by its interlocking with, and sustaining, *other* important human goods. Is this not to say, however, that these goods are instrumental to human flourishing and derive their value and importance from the Intrinsic value a good life has? In a word, no. The participation in such goods as knowledge and sociability *comprises* a human life of a certain sort. The life is not something distinct from these goods to which the goods lead, as taking an aspirin leads to relief from a headache.

What is Intrinsically good, it might be said, is a life consisting of all the important goods *in a certain structure or arrangement*. On this view, everything that is a worthy consideration in practical reasoning will be seen ultimately to derive its value from its relation to that particular structured composite of goods that comprises the ideally good human life, that thing that is good in itself. Such a view, it might be argued, is compatible with the points I have stressed about the way the importance of considerations in practical reasoning is properly determined.

It is difficult to object to the statement that living a life that combines the most important human goods in a coherent, harmonious structure is intrinsically good. Such a life would be intrinsically good because of the goods that comprise it. But if the idea that living such a life is the basic Intrinsic good is combined in a certain way with the thesis that every sound piece of practical reasoning must terminate in something that is Intrinsically good, the resulting conception of practical reasoning is objectionable. If we suppose that the test or criterion of the rightness or correctness of action is the action's conduciveness to living a certain sort of life, and if we suppose that we can articulate this goal with sufficient specificity that it will be possible quite generally in actual situations to determine which of the contemplated alternative actions is most conducive to the goal, then we will have a view of practical reasoning that has defects that are similar to the defects of the hard-and-fast-rule conception of practical reasoning. It is one thing to say that knowledge, sociability, aesthetic experience, and the rest are indispensable elements in good human life. It is quite another thing, however, to suppose that we can describe *the* ideally good human life in sufficient detail and with enough specificity that the conception could play the role of the ultimate Intrinsic good in what I will call the fixed-goal conception of practical reasoning.

On such a view, the paradigm of sound practical reasoning is choosing an effective means to a clearly defined goal. The standard of correctness of choice is conduciveness to the realization of the goal. With any practical problem concerning the general conduct of one's life — including complex moral problems involving uncertainty about the relevance of consider- ations and conflicts among considerations — the crucial question would be: which of the possible solutions most contributes to the goal of leading the ideal life? If this question is to be answerable when real problems, particularly complex ones, are involved, it is apparent that the conception of the ideal life must be in certain respects concrete and detailed. It must make clear what the goods are and what the priorities are among them. The components of this life and the relationships of these components to one another — the life's structure — must be clearly articulated. The more vague (unspecific) the conception of the goal, the ideal life, the less useful it will be in solving actual problems — that is, the fewer problems will admit of rational solution.

The fixed-goal view of practical reasoning, when it is applied to questions about the conduct of life in this way, places inor- dinate demands upon our idea of the good life. How, on the

[119]

fixed-goal view, are we to decide how the obvious candidates for important human goods are to be put together in the ideal human life? How are we to choose among the indefinitely many ways we can imagine things being fitted together? Human lives are led in concrete circumstances or contexts that vary greatly from time to time and place to place. These contexts influence enormously how lives are led; they restrict how lives can be led, how goods can be fitted together. When we attempt to describe the ideal life, in what circumstances do we suppose that the life is led? If we cannot supply *any* context at all, how are we to determine how the basic goods are to be fitted together? How are we to decide what the life's structure is? If, on the other hand, we describe the ideal life in a determinate context, how can this conception be of use to us in *other* contexts? If proper practical reasoning is a matter exclusively of choosing what most leads to this goal, what can possibly guide us in adapting the conception of a life led in one set of circumstances to our own quite different circumstances?

I do not mean to deny that it is sometimes useful to use another person's life as a guide for one's own. My point is that on the fixed-goal conception of practical reasoning, there is no provision for the *intelligent* adaptation of a conception of an ideal life described in one set of circumstances to a different set of circumstances — no hint of how the adaptation might proceed more or less reasonably. Thus, the choice of adapting the conception to my circumstances in one way rather than another will appear arbitrary. Since the matter of *how* I adapt the conception will be crucial for the decisions I then make to attain this goal, the arbitrariness will infect the decisions as well.

In constructing an account of how choices about the conduct of life are properly made, the fixed-goal theorist is faced with the fact that there are many particular good lives that are in important ways different from one another. There will be disagreements among serious people, moreover, about which of the candidates for the status of a good life are genuinely good. Puzzled by how to choose, the theorist may be tempted to look for what all such lives have in common. The description of the goal — the ideal life — can perhaps mention what is common to all particular good lives, leaving out the differences. The result of this program, however, will be a very abstract and general description of the ultimate goal of all reasonable human action — hardly the sort of determinate goal that will lead us to solutions to complex practical problems.

There is a dilemma here for the fixed-goal theorist. The more specific the description of the goal, the ideal, the more difficult it is to make plausible the claim that every right choice must advance *this* goal. Aristotle's ideal of the life of *theoria*, the contemplative life, as it is described in *Nicomachean Ethics*, Book X, Chapter 8, might be offered as an example of a *relatively* specific ideal. It is clearly less specific than a detailed biography of a life, but it is specific with respect to life's priorities — there is but one. More plausible as a claim about what the best sort of human life is like is the thesis that an active life exhibiting a variety of excellences both of character and intellect is best. There is evidence in Aristotle's writings that he thought of "the good for man" as a complex of activities in accordance with several excellences. There is, however, no indication of how Aristotle thought a conception of the good for man as a complex could be used to resolve conflicts among considerations — when, for example, one must choose between loyalty to friends and loyalty to the *polis*. A goal, described simply as "a life that combines (somehow) activity in accordance with many excellences" is too unspecific to determine what to do in situations involving conflict problems.

The modern reader of *Nicomachean Ethics* is apt to receive the impression that Aristotle wavered between the notion that the fixed goal of practical reasoning is a life of *theoria*, a life of contemplation, and the view that the fixed goal is the less specific one of a life that exhibits a variety of moral and intellectual excellences. If indeed Aristotle did waver between these

[121]

views, it may be that he was impaled upon the horns of the fixed-goal theorist's dilemma. A fixed-goal theory of practical reasoning cannot be worked out in a plausible way. This may explain why Aristotle seems not to have had a developed account of practical reasoning.

The fixed-goal conception of practical reasoning is vulnerable to the objections to the absolutist conception — the hard-and-fast-rule conception — discussed in Chapter 1. For the idea of a certain life to play the role of the ultimate Intrinsic good in a fixed-goal theory, it must be the idea of that which is, in effect, the goal promoted by the *correct* solution of every practical problem of moment — past, present, and future — concerning how human beings should live their lives. How could anyone have sufficient grounds for the claim that a certain particular conception of the ideal life meets this condition? This view, like the absolutist view, is fundamentally Platonic. The eternal, unchanging standard of correctness in action is conduciveness to a certain sort of life on the fixed-goal conception.

The vexing circularity in Aristotle's accounts of moral virtue and practical wisdom, then, is probably the result of his view of practical reasoning. It is the problem of indicating what things are *correctly* desired for their own sake that reduces him to saying that it is the things so desired by a good human being — an individual possessing the virtues — that are correctly so desired. The necessity for establishing what things are Intrinsically good, and thus properly desired for their own sake, does not arise on the contextualist, pragmatic view of practical reasoning discussed in earlier chapters. Thus, neither Aristotle's solution nor any other is required.

It MAY seem that on a pragmatist, contextualist view of practical reasoning, another sort of circularity is inescapable. Practical reasoning, on such a view, is a matter of adapting and readjusting to one another a great many ways of dealing

[122]

with a host of different problems. The things that are recognized as considerations (including goods and evils, principles, and ideals) reflect knowledge gleaned from past successes which can be expected to be of use with new problems. These considerations and their associated values do not remain fixed, however; their intelligent use continually modifies them, and such changes require further readjustments elsewhere. The value and importance of any of these things is to be understood by its relationship to other things—to the problems it solves and to the other values with which it is linked. What, though, if someone questions the value and importance of an entire system of values, of all the available ways of coping as they are at the moment in their adjustment to one another? It appears that there are only two sorts of answers possible. One can reply that the entire system is good for its own sake, and that this is self-evident. The alternative, it appears, is somehow to show that the entire system derives its value from the various goods that comprise it. Since I have repeatedly rejected appeals to self-evidence, it appears that the second alternative is the only viable one. A problem arises, however. The value and importance of a good that is a constituent of the entire system, I have said, are established by its relationships to other components of the system. If it is now claimed that the value of the whole system of goods is derived from the value of its constituents, the view is circular.

One can frame questions in such a way that no noncircular answers are possible. For example, we might ask for a justification of the set of justificatory practices that contains *all* the modes of justification. It is by no means clear what follows from the fact that such questions can be formulated.[12] If there were some problem that required us to establish the value and

12. For a discussion of such questions in the theory of knowledge, see Frederick L. Will, *Induction and Justification* (Ithaca: Cornell University Press, 1974), especially chap. 10.

importance of the whole comprised of all the values, ideals, and principles that we know, and if we attempted to establish this by pointing to the value of certain constituent goods, would the circularity of this procedure be objectionable? I do not see how this could be decided without a clear, detailed understanding of the problem and of the proposed solution. The question, posed in the abstract, is unanswerable.

A critic will point out that I am treating a philosophical requirement as if it were nothing more than a practical one. It may be, according to the critic, that in dealing with practical problems, we determine the value and importance of considerations by exploring their connections with other things, and rest content with this. A philosophical account of practical reasoning, however, must ask about the value and importance of these "other things" too. The process must continue, according to the critic, until no uncertified considerations remain in the account. My account, therefore, is not complete until it can indicate how this requirement is to be met. If I insist that the value and importance of something are generally a matter of its relationships to other things and reject the notion that these "other things" must turn out (sooner or later) to be Intrinsically good (good in themselves, desirable for their own sake), then I can meet this requirement only by showing somehow that the whole, comprised of all the goods in their relationships to one another, is Intrinsically good.

I want to reject this philosophical requirement—it is the traditional requirement that lies behind the views of Aristotle, Hume, and many others. The requirement cannot be met, and there is no good reason why it should be. The plausibility of the idea that it has to be met really depends on our supposing that the actual practice of justifying decisions rests upon the assumption that it can be met.

It is instructive to consider some remarks of R. M. Hare's on this issue.

A complete justification of a decision would consist of a complete account of its effects, together with a complete account of the principles which it observed, and the effects of observing those principles. . . . Thus, if pressed to justify a decision completely, we have to give a complete specification of the way of life of which it is a part. This complete specification it is impossible in practice to give. . . . Suppose, however, that we can give it. If the inquirer still goes on asking 'But why *should* I live like that?' then there is no further answer to give him, because we have already, *ex hypothesi*, said everything that could be included in this further answer. . . . He has to decide whether to accept that way of life or not. . . . To describe such ultimate decisions as arbitrary, because *ex hypothesi* everything which could be used to justify them has already been included in the decision, would be like saying that a complete description of the universe was utterly unfounded, because no further fact could be called upon in corroboration of it. . . . Far from being arbitrary, such a decision would be the most well-founded of decisions, because it would be based upon a consideration of everything upon which it could possibly be founded.[13]

Hare assumes at the outset that all actual justifications of decisions are inevitably and necessarily "incomplete." What lies behind this, of course, is the traditional philosophical assumption that a "complete" justification is one that leaves no room whatever for any *further* requests for justification. Thus, if I justify my decision by citing a principle that covers it, my justification is incomplete if it is then possible to ask for a justification of the principle. The philosophical view that practical reasoning should terminate in things that are Intrinsically good derives from this ideal of "complete" justification. If something is Intrinsically good, I can respond to requests for the certification of *its* value by saying, "Try it and see." That is the end of the matter. No further justification is in order, it is thought.

13. R. M. Hare, *The Language of Morals* (Oxford: Clarendon Press, 1952), p. 69.

Hare, however, does not believe in self-certifying goods or self-evident practical principles. He does think, though, that our stock of "principles"—things to appeal to in justifying decisions—is finite, although too large for anyone actually to exhaust in the course of justifying a decision. The whole stock, however, specifies an "entire way of life." If anyone were ever, in justifying a decision, to exhaust this entire stock (as no one ever does), and if he were then asked to justify living in accordance with *that* body of principles, Hare admits that no justification could be given. Any justification here would have to cite some "principle" that is a part of the specification of the way of life in question. Hare does *not* conclude, however, that the absence of a justification of the whole stock of principles renders the justification of the original decision "incomplete" in any way that renders it less than completely well founded. Yet the justification of the original decision is not "complete" in the sense of leaving nothing without a justification. What then is the relevance of this *initial* notion of completeness of justification?

It might be suggested that, from the outset, Hare means by a "complete" justification one that is "based upon everything upon which it could possibly be founded." So it is that in justifying decision D we cite principle $P1$, we justify $P1$ by $P2$, and so on until we have cited $P1$ through PN. Since by hypothesis, these are all the principles there are, the justification of D is therefore "complete"—it is based upon *everything* it could be based upon.

Why, then, is Hare so sure that if anyone *did* succeed in mentioning everything the justification of D is "based on", this would exhaust our stock of "principles" (justifying considerations)? A justification of D is "based on" or "founded on" P only if P is *relevant to* justifying D. If I justify D by citing $P1$, justify $P1$ by citing $P2$, etc., etc., justify $P275$ by citing $P276$, does it follow that $P276$ is *relevant to* justifying the original decision D? If one *assumes* that a consideration is relevant to a justification just in case it is a necessary part of a complete justification, and that a complete justification would include a justification of everything occurring in the justification, then, of course, $P276$ will be relevant to justifying decision D. It is this very notion of a "complete" justification, however, that is in question. If this notion is rejected, then there is no reason to suppose that when we show that a decision is well founded, every practical consideration there is will turn out to be relevant.

In fact, what is relevant to justifying an actual decision is determined by the concrete circumstances that call for the decision and the circumstances in which the decision is made. Relevance, here, is a notion that demands a context — relevance to the problem at hand is what concerns us in practical affairs. This traditional notion of a "complete" justification as one that includes every conceivable practical consideration is the predictable result of divorcing justification from the contexts that determine what is relevant to justification. It is not surprising that absolutely everything turns out to be relevant when the contexts that determine relevance are left out of account.

Hare describes a situation in which some individual realizes that if he asks, 'Why should I live in accordance with that set of justificatory practices that contains all the modes of justification?', no answer will be possible that does not employ the practices in question. The individual must simply decide, when faced by such a question, Hare says, whether to live in accordance with that set of procedures. This is described as though it is simply a decision about whether to opt for one way of life as opposed to another very different one. We think of Paul Gauguin's decision to live among the natives of Tahiti, or we imagine a university professor, tired of complexity and continual adversarial encounters with others, considering whether to become a Buddhist monk or to live among the Maya of Quintana Roo. These analogies, however, are most misleading. Deciding is a practice we have learned. Gauguin and the

[127]

imaginary university professor, however radical the changes in way of life they contemplate, are, in deciding, engaging in a practice they have learned — making decisions. They seek some situation in which certain features of their past life that seem to them desirable are retained while other undesirable features are less prominent or excluded altogether. What Hare's imaginary individual is doing, however, is "deciding" but not having recourse to any practices he has learned. It is as if we are to imagine him walking without moving his body. The philosophical point here, which is supposed to be distinct from practical points, maintains its appearance of making sense only when it is confused with practical points from which it is distinct.

THE BELIEF that it is essential to justify our entire way of life — to certify as correct all our standards of justification — is related to one of the oldest and most powerful motives for engaging in philosophical reflection. The fact is that there exist other ways of life, in the form of other cultures with norms and standards that differ from ours. This state of affairs seems to challenge us to show the superiority of our own ways over the others. Here, in the words of historian William McNeill, is a concrete example of a conflict between two different cultures that evokes this reaction. In 1839, in China,

> a British sailor committed murder; and when the guilty individual could not be identified, the Chinese, in accordance with their practice of holding the community responsible for infractions of law and order, demanded that an Englishman — any Englishman — be turned over to them for punishment. No apter instance of the conflict between European and Chinese outlooks could have offered itself; for both sides naturally felt themselves completely in the right. [14]

14. William McNeill, *The Rise of the West* (Chicago: University of Chicago Press, 1963), p. 717n. A different account of this incident is to be

The British, of course, were shocked and indignant at the Chinese demand and rejected it. The Chinese, in response, were angered and offended by the British refusal to assume responsibility in the manner the Chinese thought appropriate. The result of this incident was violence, with British gunboats and marines proving their military superiority.

For a Westerner, justice clearly requires that individuals not be punished for offenses committed by others; the Chinese demand is outrageous. This is a fundamental requirement of justice, and our judicial system is built upon it. This requirement, one would expect, supports and sustains a variety of important features of our ways. In these terms, we can understand the importance and value of the requirement. It is unlikely, however, that this requirement could similarly be justified in terms of Chinese ways and values. A typical reaction to such considerations is to feel that our justification of our notions of justice in terms of our own traditions and practices is called into question by the existence of other ways in terms of which our notions of justice might not be justifiable. This is not an altogether reasonable reaction. It does not follow from the fact that other peoples have come to terms with their problems by developing certain ways that are different from ours that there is anything wrong with their ways or ours. Their histories, circumstances, and problems will have been different from ours, and their ways *may be* as well adapted to their circumstances as our ways are to our circumstances. The sort of cultural relativism involved in the view I am advocating does not undermine the possibility of intellectually satisfying justifications of certain of our practices in terms of our circumstances, our commitments, our way of life. There is no neces-

---

found in Immanuel C. Y. Hsu, *The Rise of Modern China* (New York: Oxford University Press, 1970), p. 230. The incident was a precipitating factor of the Opium Wars.

sity here, then, to search for some extracultural supernorm by which to certify collectively all our ways and values.

Does not the sort of relativism to which I am committed imply that such intercultural disputes as the one that followed upon the murder by the British sailor cannot be resolved by rational means? On the contrary, its recognition removes a serious obstacle to a constructive approach to such problems. A realization by both parties to such a dispute that the cause of their disagreement is rooted in fundamental differences in their ways of life and that neither party is going to be able simply to adopt the other's view, is necessary for them to have any chance of solving their problem. A mutual search for a solution that somehow satisfies to a degree the requirements of both parties is a reasonable course for disputants who wish to solve the problem without resorting to force. The British could have accepted the point that when a member of their navy or merchant marine commits murder in a foreign country, they bear a responsibility to respond to the complaint of the host nation. They cannot turn over an innocent Englishman to be punished, and they can explain why this is impossible for them. They can, however, accept the responsibility somehow to compensate the host nation, and if the Chinese should be willing to regard this as punishment for the crime, then a solution without violence might be possible.

I hope it is clear that the relativism implicit in the view I advocate does not imply that a practice is shown to be a good one by the fact that it is widely accepted in a community. There may be practices that have been accepted in some communities which would be bad practices in any community we know of. The vendetta seems to me such a practice. Perhaps a more interesting candidate is slavery. A slave is subject in all matters to the arbitrary will of a master and is held in contempt by that master. Such circumstances provide a fertile ground for the growth of deep resentment and hatred of the master on the part of the slave. It seems in some sense possible that masters might always treat their slaves with kindness and that slaves might accept their situation with equanimity, but there is reason to believe that in fact this does not happen. On the basis of a careful study of slavery in scores of societies, Orlando Patterson concludes, "There is absolutely no evidence from the long and dismal annals of slavery to suggest that any group of slaves ever internalized the conception of degradation held by their masters. To be dishonored — and to sense, however acutely, such dishonor — is not to lose the quintessential human urge to participate and to want a place."[15]

Slaves are always powerless relative to their masters, and such a condition of powerlessness is incompatible with honor or dignity. Masters accept this view of their slaves, but in fact slaves do not. In commenting upon this point of Patterson's, Michael Walzer says:

> The whole point of enslavement . . . is radically to degrade and dishonor the slave, to deny him a social place, a "stage of his own." Slaves, in the eyes of their masters, are base, irresponsible, shameless, infantile. They can be whipped or petted, but they cannot, in the proper sense of the words, be praised or blamed. Their value is the price they command at auction, and they are denied any other value or any recognition of value. But they do not themselves participate in this denial. . . . Slaves and masters do not inhabit a world of shared meanings. The two groups are simply at war.[16]

Such profound degradation of a group in a community creates a community full of enemies. A community with an institution of slavery is therefore a community at war with itself. There is reason, then, to think that slavery is a bad institution in any community.[17]

15. Orlando Patterson, *Slavery and Social Death* (Cambridge: Harvard University Press, 1982), p. 97.
16. Walzer, *Spheres of Justice*, p. 250n.
17. Compare this with Aristotle's argument against excluding from a share

There are transcultural values, including human goods and evils, that are based upon the biological nature of human beings. Biologically, we are social organisms, and our welfare depends upon community. There are certain *sine qua non* conditions for society, and the divisive effects of slavery tend to undercut those. Such abstract considerations as we find in these transcultural goods and evils, however, will not provide us with means of coping with practical problems in the form in which they present themselves. Walzer makes this point in discussing distributive justice.

> There is no single set of primary or basic goods conceivable across all moral and material worlds—or, any such set would have to be conceived in terms so abstract that they would be of little use in thinking about particular distributions. Even the range of necessities, if we take into account moral as well as physical necessities, is very wide, and the rank orderings are very different. A single necessary good, and one that is always necessary—food, for example—carries different meanings in different places. Bread is the staff of life, the body of Christ, the symbol of the Sabbath, the means of hospitality, and so on.[18]

ON THE pragmatist, contextualist view of practical reasoning, there is no reason to suppose that any practical problem requires for its solution that we show the value and importance of the whole comprised of *all* our resources for solving practical problems, including values, ideals, and principles. If

---

of power in a *polis* "the general body of citizens" who have neither wealth nor excellence: "A state with a body of disenfranchised citizens who are numerous and poor must necessarily be a state which is full of enemies" (*Politics*, 1281b 29–31). The translation is that of Ernest Barker in *The Politics of Aristotle* (Oxford: Clarendon Press, 1946).

18. Walzer, *Spheres of Justice*, p. 8.

someone claims to intuit the Intrinsic value and reasonableness of the entire body of our ways of coping in practical matters, it must be made clear that what is thereby "certified" is our collective practical wisdom *such as it is* — warts and all. It is not a thing that has attained (or can attain) some form of final perfection. It will change and readjust as it always has — sometimes, we may hope, for the better. Common sense would dictate that any serious attempt to assess our *current* intellectual resources for dealing with practical matters proceed by an examination of what our pressing problems are and how well we cope with them.

[5]

The End of a Life:
A Relevance Problem

WE ARE sometimes confronted with situations in which the relevance of a certain moral consideration is unclear and controverted. When a situation is unprecedented and is in significant ways both like and unlike familiar cases where the moral consideration clearly does apply, we are apt to be puzzled. When the novelty of the case is such that it is unclear whether the words we use to formulate the consideration apply or not, and when the circumstances are such that some action is required, we have a difficult moral problem. The issues involved are apt to be clearly recognizable philosophical issues.

I have not yet discussed moral relevance problems in any detail. It is evident, however, that such problems are sometimes of the greatest importance, and that most ethical theories do not treat them in a way that is useful to us in understanding them. We should reject the notion that there already exist (somehow, somewhere) moral principles or decision procedures that simply tell us how to solve such problems. These problems are paradigmatic of ones for which we must create solutions, using ingenuity and whatever intellectual resources we have.

[134]

How, though, can such problems be resolved reasonably *and* in a way that provides solutions faithful to existing ideals and commitments? The following well-worn example bears certain similarities to these puzzling cases. You are a police officer in a jurisdiction with a century-old statute barring wheeled vehicles in the park. Coming toward you, as you patrol the park, is a child on a skateboard. Is this a violation of the statute? Is a skateboard a "wheeled vehicle" in the sense those words have in the formulation of the statute? In other words, is the statute relevant in this instance? It is reasonable to ask what the purpose or point of the statute is; the answer may be of help. If, for example, the whole point of the statute is to protect the paths in the park from damage from wheels, then, so far, there is probably reason to maintain that a skateboard is not a wheeled vehicle in the sense of the statute.

Moral considerations, unless they are senseless taboos, have points, purposes too. In moral problems where the relevance of a certain moral consideration is problematic, it is often useful for us to reflect upon the point or points of the consideration. With what sort of difficulties has the consideration been of use in the past? The result of such reflections may enable us to make an intellectually satisfying case for the consideration's relevance or irrelevance to the situation, and this may solve the problem. Such moral problems are often very difficult; I am not suggesting that there is a surefire way to easy solutions. Complex problems involving sufficiently novel situations do not admit of mechanical solutions. Rather, I am suggesting that this idea provides a useful hint about how we can proceed in the difficult task of seeking reasoned solutions to moral relevance problems.

The central issue in the current controversy about the definition of death can fruitfully be regarded as a moral relevance problem. The problem is complex and difficult, but it can be treated in the way just described. In what follows, I will pursue the idea that in a certain circumstance, a human life is, in at least one important respect, like a wheeled vehicle. These are alike, I will maintain, in that in the context of a certain problem, we can gain insight into what these things are by considering why they are of practical concern.

FOR CENTURIES, the criterion of the death of a human being has been the permanent cessation of "vital signs"—of respiration, heartbeat, and the circulation of the blood. Recently, however, means have been developed for mechanically sustaining vital functions after the cessation of spontaneous functioning. By such means, the breathing and heartbeat of irreversibly comatose individuals sometimes can be sustained for days or even weeks. Because of the great expense of such sustenance and because of the demand for certain organs for transplantation, there is considerable support for the view that machines sustaining vital functions should be turned off in such cases and organs removed as needed elsewhere.

The following thought, however, is arresting. To cause the permanent cessation of a person's vital functions is to bring about the death of that individual.[1] The moral permissibility of removing a life-support device can be established only if we can show that it is all right to act so as to bring about the death of an innocent, totally helpless human being. Comatose individuals cannot be consulted, nor can they be said to be suffering, so it will not be easy to justify bringing about their deaths. The suggestion that we adopt the practice of bringing about the deaths of certain helpless human beings to save money or to provide organs for other people is a disturbing one. Viewed

---

1. I am using the phrase 'bringing about *N*'s death' to mean *either* killing *N* or letting *N* die. For my purposes, nothing hangs on the question of whether causing the permanent cessation of *N*'s vital functions is actively to kill *N* or passively to let *N* die.

in this light, the moral permissibility of turning off machinery that sustains the vital functions of such people is problematic.

In response to such misgivings, it is proposed that death be redefined in such a way that certain irreversibly comatose individuals whose breathing and so on can be sustained only artificially are regarded as dead.[2] There can be no question of bringing about the death of certain irreversibly comatose individuals by causing the permanent cessation of their vital functions if they are already dead. A question that needs to be answered, however, is this: How can redefining death in this way remove the substantive grounds for moral objections to causing the permanent cessation of breathing and other vital functions in innocent, helpless human beings? In the absence of a convincing answer to this question, the following charge is troubling: The proposal to redefine death in such a way that certain irreversibly comatose individuals are counted as "dead" may help us to hide from ourselves the wrongness of bringing about the death of such people, but it does not alter the wrongness of the act.

The central issue in this problem can be described as follows. We are morally required not to kill innocent, helpless human beings and to preserve such lives where we can. Are these requirements *relevant* to the question of whether it is all right to discontinue the mechanical support of the vital processes of the irreversibly comatose when this will lead to the permanent cessation of those processes? If there are reasons to suppose that some or all of these individuals really are dead,

2. See "A Definition of Irreversible Coma: Report of the Ad Hoc Committee of the Harvard Medical School to Examine the Definition of Brain Death," *Journal of the American Medical Association* 205 (1968), 337–340. A survey of current thinking on this and related issues can be found in the report of the President's Commission for the Study of Ethical Problems in Medicine and Biomedical and Behavioral Research entitled *Defining Death: Medical, Legal and Ethical Issues in the Determination of Death* (Washington, D.C.: U.S. Government Printing Office, 1981). This last work is cited hereafter as *Defining Death*.

[137]

then there is an argument that supports the claim that moral requirements to protect and preserve human life do not apply, are not relevant in such cases. It is necessary to show, however, that in redefining death in such a way that certain comatose individuals are dead, we are not merely arbitrarily stipulating that they are dead. The proposed redefinition must be shown to be grounded in the real nature of death if it is to support the claim that the requirements that we protect and preserve human life are not relevant in these cases.

ALTHOUGH THERE is a strong consensus that includes people of diverse moral, political, and religious views in favor of this redefinition, there is no agreement on the grounds for the redefinition. Many of the arguments designed to justify it appear question-begging. Scientists discussing this issue have a tendency to treat death as purely a physiological phenomenon, neglecting its place in human affairs generally. It is argued, for example, that death should be regarded as primarily a matter of permanent cessation of brain-function rather than permanent cessation of respiration and heartbeat because the brain's function is to regulate and organize the functioning of the body's major organ systems. The brain, according to the president's commission to study such matters, is "the regulator of the body's integration."

> Breathing and heartbeat are not life itself. They are simply used as signs — as one window for viewing a deeper and more complex reality: A triangle of interrelated systems with the brain at its apex. . . . Since life is a matter of integrating the functioning of major organ systems, breathing and circulation are necessary but not sufficient to establish that an individual is alive. When an individual's breathing and circulation lack neurologic integration, he or she is dead.[3]

3. *Defining Death*, p. 33.

[138]

Why, though, should we take "neurologic integration" to be life itself? How is this point established unless its proponents have already shown that individuals are dead whose brains have ceased functioning but whose respiration and heartbeat are sustained mechanically?

> The view that the brain's functions are more central to "life" than those of the skin, the liver, and so on, is admittedly arbitrary in the sense of representing a choice. The view is not, however, arbitrary in the sense of lacking reasons. As discussed previously, the centrality accorded the brain reflects both its overarching role as "regulator" or "integrator" of other bodily systems and the immediate and devastating consequences of its loss for the organism as a whole. Furthermore, the Commission believes that this choice overwhelmingly reflects the views of experts and the lay public alike.[4]

The reasons given for this "choice" are not compelling. The loss of functioning of any one of a number of bodily organs is grievous—devastating. With the loss of the regulating, integrating function of the brain, however, it is possible by artificial means to keep the remaining bodily systems functioning for days or even weeks. Why should not an individual with such impaired bodily functioning be regarded as alive, although incapacitated and dying? The suggestion that the brain is a "regulator" and thus stands at the "apex" of the system of normally functioning organs does not explain why an individual is not alive who retains other functions with mechanical aid without the brain as regulator. That there is an emerging consensus that people with irreversible loss of brain-function are dead is suggestive, but it does not help us to see why this is a reasonable view.[5]

4. *Defining Death*, p. 35.
5. For further discussion of some biological arguments for this redefinition, see Michael B. Green and Daniel Wikler, "Brain Death and Personal

The view *is* a reasonable one, and to see why this is so, we must enlarge our view to include more than physiology. The death of a human being is the terminus of that individual's life. One's death marks the end of one's career as a human being. It is important to emphasize the adjective 'human' in talking about the end of a human life. For one thing, many people, while recognizing the occurrence of death, believe that we survive our deaths. On such a view, at death, our careers as human beings are ended, at least until by divine intervention our human bodies are reconstituted and reanimated. There is another reason why it must be kept in mind that we are concerned with the end of a *human* life. It is well known that the body of a dead human being may contain living tissue and living cells. Being a living human being is not merely a matter of a certain proportion of the cells in a human body being *living cells*. We are not just colonies of living cells.

As biologists well know, life comes in different forms, and the form of life characteristic of a cell is different from the form of life characteristic of human beings. When a certain sort of body possesses a capacity to carry on the activities that are characteristic of the human form of life, then we have a living human being.[6] The form of life characteristic of human beings is a complicated form of social life. A survey of our kind reveals that everywhere human life involves community, language, art, morality, politics, and cumulative knowledge, among other things. The capacities, physical and psychological, for living this form of life are many. Human beings learn the ways of their community, absorb whatever store of wisdom the community has, learn to adapt this store to their own particular circumstances and projects, and attempt to conduct their lives in accordance with all these things. A human being's partici-

---

Identity," *Philosophy and Public Affairs* 9 (1980), 105–114.

6. This is an adaptation of Aristotle's definition of *psuche* ("soul"). See *De Anima*, Book II, chaps. 1–3.

pating in this form of life, the exercise of those capacities the possession of which is living, consists of episodes of doing and experiencing. One's life is a drama in which one is the protagonist. When the doings and experiences which make the drama end finally, one's life is over.

When a human being is *irreversibly* comatose, the individual is incapable of any further participation in human life whatsoever—the individual is permanently incapable of any doings or experiences. Such a person's life has ended; the individual is dead. Since "brain death" is a highly reliable indicator of irreversible coma, this is an appropriate indicator of death.[7]

How, though, does this sort of justification for the proposed redefinition of death escape the charge that it begs the question of whether the irreversibly comatose are dead? If the account just given of the nature of human life and its terminus captures the basic core idea of death, then it is apparent that the revised criterion of death is more nearly congruent with the core notion than is the traditional "vital signs" criterion. Who is to say, however, that "vital signs" is not the central conception here? What shows that it is a mistake to think that a living human being is but a breathing human body with a beating heart?

It is tempting at this point to argue in the following way. We are concerned to establish when a *person* dies. When the person, Mary Jones, becomes irreversibly comatose, that person ceases to exist and thus is dead. In support of this, consider that mackerels, cockatoos, and pigs fail to qualify as persons because they lack certain psychological capacities that you and I have. But the irreversibly comatose individual lacks these same capacities. Thus, the person dies upon becoming irreversibly comatose.

It will suffice to make one point about this argument. There is a sense in which it is obviously true that a person is essen-

7. "A Definition of Irreversible Coma," and *Defining Death*, pp. 24–26.

tially a being with certain psychical capacities. It does not follow from this, however, that a *mutilated* or *damaged person* might not lack these capacities. It is true by definition that an ungulate is a mammal with hooves, but it is also true that a horse whose hooves have been chopped off is a *mutilated ungulate*. These essential characteristics of persons and ungulates are necessary characteristics of normal, mature specimens of the kind. Normal mature persons (and human beings) necessarily possess certain intellectual capacities. Immature, damaged, and mutilated persons, however, *may* lack these capacities. So human infants are regarded as persons — not persons *simpliciter*, but as immature persons.[8] We know, then, that an irreversibly comatose human being is not a normal person. We do not yet know, however, whether or not such an individual is a grievously damaged (living) person.

Michael B. Green and Daniel Wikler argue that it follows from a certain philosophical account of personal identity that when we permanently lose all our psychical capacities, we cease to exist and thus die.[9] The account of personal identity upon which this argument is based, however, is by no means generally accepted. Like other accounts of the topic, it is supported by claims about what we would believe about the identity of persons involved in certain purely fictional extraordinary happenings — cases of brain transplantation from one body to another, "body switching," and the like. W. V. Quine remarked about such accounts, "The method of science fiction has its uses in philosophy, but . . . I wonder whether the limits of the

---

8. There are moral requirements that protect the lives of persons. It is sometimes argued that a human fetus is not protected by such requirements because it lacks the capacities essential to normal adult persons. This involves an *ignoratio elenchi*, because 'person' in the formulation of these requirements is understood to apply to immature and damaged persons too. A relevant question is whether a fetus qualifies as an immature person, but this is not addressed. See, for example, Mary Anne Warren, "On the Moral and Legal Status of Abortion," *The Monist* 57 (1973), 43–61.

9. Green and Wikler, "Brain Death and Personal Identity," pp. 117–126.

method are properly heeded. To seek what is 'logically required' for sameness of person under unprecedented circumstances is to suggest that words have some logical force beyond what our past needs have invested them with."[10] Derek Parfit quotes this passage and dismisses it on the grounds that we in fact do find ourselves reacting with strong beliefs about such purely imaginary cases.[11]

This response of Parfit's, however, does not address Quine's point. Our present intellectual resources, including our "concepts," were developed in dealing with our past experience, our past problems. Unprecedented occurrences will require us to modify these resources in order to deal with questions and problems posed by the unprecedented cases. Suppose we write a science fiction story in which people's living bodies on earth are destroyed and identical living bodies are assembled out of new materials on a distant planet. The newly created bodies are animated by personalities identical with those of their former earthly counterparts, and these individuals have detailed recollections of their counterparts' lives on earth. Suppose we believe strongly that these are the same people who formerly lived on earth. What does this show about our present notion of personal identity? We might claim that *if* such extraordinary things were to occur, it would be reasonable for us to extend and alter our ideas about personal identity in such a way that people undergoing such changes would be regarded as the same individuals. This does not show, however, that our present concept of personal identity is identical with the one it would be reasonable to adopt if such things started to happen. Quite different unprecedented occurrences could require *other* extensions and alterations of our present notions that would be *contrary* to the ones that would be reasonable in response to the

10. W. V. Quine, "Review of Milton K. Munitz, ed., *Identity and Individuation*," *Journal of Philosophy* 69 (1972), 490.
11. Parfit, *Reasons and Persons*, p. 200.

first imaginary case. Even if we have beliefs about imaginary cases, it does not follow that the concepts devised to deal with these cases are the ones we presently have, or that such modifications should be adopted in a world where such things do not happen.

How seriously should we take the belief that in a certain purely imaginary case in which some extraordinary thing happens to a person, the person remains (or does not remain) the same person? Unprecedented cases, when we actually encounter them, can pose *very* difficult problems. They sometimes have surprising ramifications that we could not have foreseen which turn out to affect in important respects the ways we adapt to deal with these cases. It is difficult to anticipate what will be relevant to our decisions in such cases. If we are dealing with descriptions of purely imaginary cases, these descriptions may be indeterminate in respects that would turn out to be decisive in answering the questions that puzzle us. Without knowing ahead of time how to answer these questions, we could hardly be sure that our descriptions of imaginary cases contain what would be relevant to answering the questions. Our strong beliefs about imaginary cases may be simply reactions to incomplete descriptions — descriptions that leave undetermined crucial matters that would affect our beliefs.

Quine's point is that the practice of philosophers who defend views of personal identity by appeal to what we believe about purely imaginary cases is unsatisfactory. I believe he is right about this.

In the next section, I will defend the claim that the individual who is known to be irreversibly comatose and who at the same time exhibits vital signs is an unprecedented case. Our present intellectual resources, including our conceptions of ourselves and beliefs about the world, cannot *in their present form* determine for us whether these individuals are dead. These, of course, are not purely imaginary cases. Suppose, however, that John Jones believes strongly that Mary Jones — lying brain-dead with her vital signs sustained—is Mary Jones alive but most grievously damaged. The news that a certain account of personal identity, based upon claims about extraordinary fictional cases, implies that this cannot be Mary Jones would not and should not change the mind of John Jones. If John Jones's belief is true, this account of personal identity is mistaken. The account of personal identity appears to beg the question about whether this is Mary Jones, terribly injured but alive.[12]

WHAT MUST be kept in mind in thinking about the proposal to redefine death in the present circumstances is this: Heretofore, as far as we knew, permanent cessation of "vital signs" was the only sufficiently reliable criterion for the permanent loss of the capacity for doings and experiences. The two ideas were thus joined in our concept of human death; for millennia, the two sorts of cessations were taken to be the same event. Recently, however, there have been changes in what we know and what we can do. We have discovered additional ways of determining that an individual's capacity for doings and experiences is permanently gone. The brain-death criterion for irreversible coma is such a test. Moreover, it is now possible to sustain breathing and heartbeat in brain-dead individuals for significant periods of time. The effect of these developments is to drive a wedge between permanent cessation of "vital signs" and permanent loss of the capacity for doings and experiences. Formerly, as far as we knew, these things were always conjoined. Now, however, we have in certain circumstances separated them; we can sustain "vital signs" in some individuals who are *known* to be irreversibly comatose. Our idea of death

---

12. The sort of defense of the brain-death criterion offered by Green and Wikler is criticized—with justice, I think— for importing problematic philosophical theses about identity into the already vexed issue of when a life ends. See *Defining Death*, pp. 39–40.

is fractured, and we must decide which of the two fragments is henceforth in such circumstances to be regarded as death.

To view the proponents of the brain-death definition in this dispute as conceptual innovators and proponents of the "vital signs" definition as defenders of the status quo misrepresents the situation. The individuals who are *known* to be irreversibly comatose *and* whose "vital signs" are sustained are unprecedented cases. Whether we decide in the end that such individuals are dead or that they are alive, the traditional notion of death will be changed. Neither of the choices is properly regarded as a choice for the traditional notion, and neither of the sides in this dispute can claim that since it defends the traditional notion, the burden of proof lies with the other side.

If we conceive of the moral requirements that protect human life as the passive conception of reasonableness in following rules would have us understand them, then these moral requirements are useless in cases such as these. No existing formulations of moral requirements can be expected simply to tell us what to do with breathing individuals who are known to be irreversibly comatose. On this conception, we seem to be forced to say that this is a medical problem, a scientific problem, not a moral problem. If only the scientists would tell us what death is or when a human being is dead, then we could say with confidence whether a brain-dead individual is alive or dead. Scientists and physicians, however, apparently are no better prepared to cope with this issue than anyone else. If they wish to address the sort of thing we are concerned with when we want to know whether a "brain-dead" human being is a dead human being, they too must face the fact that the conception of death is fractured in the way described.

A decision must be made whether, in the case of individuals known to be irreversibly comatose whose "vital signs" are sustained, death is constituted by permanent cessation of consciousness or permanent cessation of "vital signs." When the matter is put this way, it is apparent, I think, what decision is supported by the stronger reasons. The preponderance of concerns that we have with death — practical, emotional, and moral — lies with the permanent and complete cessation of a human being's capacity for doing and experiencing. This is not to deny that we might have strong feelings about extinguishing the "vital functions" of an irreversibly comatose individual. These feelings, however, can be regarded as the persistence of old habits of thinking and feeling established before we knew of cases where the two sorts of permanent cessation of capacity were sundered.

What is required is that we reshape our idea of death in a way that minimizes the disruption occasioned by the change. Continuity is sustained if we understand what the importance is of the "fragments" of the original idea, and are guided by that knowledge in doing the reshaping. There are no a priori limits to the sorts of importance that might be relevant. Theoretical considerations known best to scientists *might* have indicated that we should redefine death in one way rather than another. My point is that there appear to be no scientific considerations that settle the question in this particular case, whereas there are a variety of practical considerations (broadly speaking) that do settle the matter.

To support the claim that the preponderance of concerns that we have with the terminus of a human life are connected with the permanent cessation of the capacity of consciousness rather than the cessation of "vital signs," we can consider the point (or points) of the moral requirements for protecting and preserving human life. The moral requirements that protect human life are taken very seriously indeed, and the legal penalties for homicide are among the most severe. Why are we so concerned about human lives and their protection? Why are these matters of such importance to us? What is required here is an explanation of the practical importance of human lives, and explanation will be found in the relationships of lives to other things that concern us. The project of composing an appreciation of the importance of human life could be a pro-longed and elaborate undertaking. It will suffice for present purposes, however, to say enough to support the proposed redefinition of death. At least some of the rationales for our concern for life are obvious.

To begin with, the cooperative form of social life that is community life requires that people trust one another in certain ways to help one another and not to do harm. Planning for the future and the willingness to commit time and resources to cooperative ventures presupposes a degree of security. Each individual is to a degree protected by requirements that we protect and preserve human life and thus has a stake in them. These requirements help sustain and promote conditions of mutual trust and security that are necessary for the sort of community life that is characteristically human.

There are, too, other, deeper reasons for our valuing human life as we do and supporting requirements that we protect and preserve it. A human community, as Aristotle saw, is not just a trade association or an organization for mutual protection. People in a community share a language, a morality, a culture. Such sharing — sharing a way of life — requires common expectations, aspirations, standards, and values. Such mutuality, such sharing, would be peculiar, to say the least, if the individuals were indifferent to one another, if they had no concern for one another's welfare. A concern for the welfare of the community as a whole could not exist if the members of the community were mutually indifferent. Since a person's being alive is, except in extraordinary circumstances, a crucial component of his or her welfare, people's concern for one another will embrace a willingness to protect and preserve one another's lives. In a world where people from different communities increasingly attempt to live together, the argument for the desirability of generalizing this concern to all human beings is increasingly powerful.

[148]

Mutual concern among the members of a human community will be an important factor in any such community, but, of course, the practices of different communities in this regard vary. This should not be surprising. Local conditions will differ, and different communities will have faced different problems. Some communities, moreover, will have developed better ways than others of coping and of living together.

John Rawls writes eloquently of the importance of self-respect and self-esteem. "Without [self-respect] nothing may seem worth doing, or if some things have value for us, we lack the will to strive for them. All desire and activity becomes empty and vain, and we sink into apathy and cynicism."[13] Our morale and self-esteem require that we believe that our own life is important and that our projects and our efforts to execute them are important too. Yet the lives, the projects and activities, of our fellows are not all that different from our own. If we deny the worth of others' lives, by implication we depreciate our own. When we as a community express our collective (shared) appreciation of the value of human life by requiring of one another that we forbear from killing and take action to preserve lives, we express to each our appreciation of his or her importance. These requirements can be regarded as expressions of our concern for every person and of our support for the view that each is important.

We would appeal to such considerations as these if we were set the task of showing that there is good reason for us as a community to require, as we do, that we forbear from killing one another and that we strive to preserve the lives of others even at cost to ourselves. These considerations show us the point of our attitude toward human life and our practices with respect to it.

Some lives are incomplete, truncated because of the absence or impairment of certain capacities necessary for leading fully

13. Rawls, *A Theory of Justice*, p. 440.

the form of life characteristic of our kind. Human lives that are defective in this way are, in our view, as worthy of protection and preservation as nondefective ones. We see in such lives the features that make our own lives valuable. These are, like us, people with goals and aspirations; they are also people with terrible problems. Moreover, we know that each of us may at any moment become incomplete, incapacitated in some more or less catastrophic way. Not only does each individual's security and trust of his fellows depend upon his confidence that we protect and preserve one another, but the concern for the welfare of one another that is such an important part of the fabric of our social life dictates that we help our incapacitated fellows.

These considerations shed light on the problem of revising our idea of when a human life is over. From an understanding of the point of protecting human life, we gain a perspective upon what is important about human life. This perspective enables us to establish what is central and what is peripheral here. In order to compare the general importance of the capacity for doing and experiencing with that of the capacity for vital functions (with or without mechanical assistance), consider the following two policies.

> A. We permanently extinguish the capacity for doing and experiencing in human beings when the maintenance of an individual is burdensome.
> B. We permanently extinguish the capacity for vital functions in individuals who are known by reliable tests to be irreversibly comatose when such maintenance is burdensome.

The same reasons that we found for requirements that we protect and preserve human life would clearly be reasons for rejecting policy A. Policy A, if adopted, would undermine mutual trust among people, it would require us to harden ourselves quite generally toward the aspirations and welfare of others, and it would require us to accept a distinctly lower appraisal of everyone's importance and worth, including our own. The points, the functions of our moral requirements protecting and preserving human life would be very appreciably undermined by the adoption of policy A. This cannot be said about the adoption of policy B.

What can be said against adopting policy B, apart from the question-begging contention that it licenses homicide? When I consider destroying the life that remains in the cells and tissues of an irreversibly comatose individual, I do not contemplate destroying anything whose destruction *in me* in similar circumstances I would have reason to oppose. By contrast, I have a plethora of reasons for opposing the permanent destruction of my capacity for doing and experiencing. Of course, one *might* desire that after one's consciousness had ceased permanently, one's vital systems continue functioning as long as possible. One cannot, however, muster reasons for this desire that even begin to approach the gravity of the reasons one has for wanting one's capacity for doing and experiencing to continue. The latter is the foundation for the enjoyment of all other goods of life. It is the cornerstone of one's welfare. Thus, should we adopt policy A, we are in important ways failing to show a concern for the general welfare — all the interests — of the individuals whose consciousness is permanently extinguished. The adoption of policy B can at most frustrate the wishes of individuals about what happens to their bodies after they have ceased to be capable of any conscious functions. Such wishes have no more and no less importance than do people's wishes about how their remains are to be treated after death: there is a point in respecting such wishes, but not when so doing imposes heavy burdens on others. In adopting policy B and applying it even to people who are on record as wanting their vital functions sustained when they become irreversibly comatose, we do not show anything like the wholesale disregard of others' interests and welfare that would be shown by the adoption of policy A. Furthermore, our general trust in one another and hope for mutual aid is not undermined by the adoption of policy B. The practice is apparently compatible with mutual respect, concern, and love for one another as profound as one would like.

What these reflections show is that the moral requirements that we protect and preserve human life are not concerned primarily with protecting a colony of living cells or a system of functioning organs; rather they are meant to protect the protagonist in a drama that is that individual's life.[14] This life consists in intermittent episodes of activities and experiences. When the capacity for such episodes is gone, so that they cease permanently, there is no point in applying the requirements of protecting and preserving human life.

I anticipate the following objection. "If there is no point in applying these requirements to the irreversibly comatose, then this is an argument for not applying them in such cases. It does not follow from the inapplicability of the requirements, however, that the irreversibly comatose are dead. We could, then, quite reasonably view the irreversibly comatose as living, as long as they manifest 'vital signs,' and amend the rules about killing and letting die to make it explicit that such individuals are exceptions."

I agree, of course, that the above considerations show that our moral requirements that one protect and preserve human life should not be applied to the irreversibly comatose. I am claiming further, however, that *in the present circumstances*, we

---

14. In chapter 15 of *After Virtue*, Alasdair MacIntyre maintains that the unity of a self or person and whatever unity a person's life has are the sort of unity we find in narratives—stories or histories. It may seem strange to claim that such basic unities are aesthetic in character, but the idea can be made plausible. In *Art as Experience*, John Dewey develops the idea that aesthetic qualities, which artists strive to embody in their works, are heightened and intensified instances of certain of the most basic and important qualities of our ordinary experience. This unfortunately neglected theory is of considerable philosophical interest.

must redefine death. The relevant circumstances are: Two closely associated ideas of human life and its terminus have been separated by the unprecedented case of the individual who is *known* to be irreversibly comatose *and* who manifests "vital signs." In answering the question, are such individuals alive or dead?, we change our idea of death. The only question is, for which redefinition can the stronger case be made? The account of why there is no point in applying the moral requirements in the case of the irreversibly comatose shows that the idea of a human being capable of doing and experiencing is more central to the notion of human life than is the idea of a human body manifesting "vital signs." *What* we value, *what* we are concerned with in our concern with human life, is shown to be the capacity for doing and experiencing. This is the important thing. The concerns with human life that are expressed in moral requirements of its protection and preservation are focused upon the individual capable of doing and experiencing. All that can be said for counting the irreversibly comatose as alive is that we are accustomed to thinking of human bodies that manifest "vital signs" as living human beings. This habit, however, derives from our long experience of the permanent cessation of "vital signs" as the only reliable indicator of the permanent cessation of the capacity for doing and experiencing. The preponderance of reason, then, supports redefining death in such a way that those known to be irreversibly comatose are dead.[15]

Another objection to the argument that I have offered for a particular redefinition of death is this. "The argument focuses upon what is peculiar to *human* life. In effect, it is argued that when the peculiarly *human* feature is gone, then life is gone

15. Note that I am not appealing here to any such premise as, "If a thing of a certain kind loses its value, it ceases to be a thing of that kind." As Green and Wikler point out in criticizing certain moral arguments for adopting the brain-death definition, such a general premise is false. See "Brain Death and Personal Identity," pp. 115–116.

too. Life, however, is a natural condition shared by other species of animals and all species of plants. What is peculiarly human in human life need not be essential to its being *life*."

It is true that life occurs in certain kinds of creatures who are incapable of doings and experiences. (I do not claim that only human beings are capable of doings and experiences.) Does this imply, however, that it is a mistake to define death in human beings in such a way that conclusive indication that the capacity for such things is completely and permanently lost is necessary and sufficient for death? Does the fact that there are kinds of living creatures that are incapable of breathing and heartbeat imply that it is a mistake to define human death as the permanent cessation of "vital signs"?

It is undeniable that human life is continuous with that of all kinds of living creatures, but the continuity is such that my claims about death are consistent with it. Life comes in different forms. Being alive, for a certain kind of creature, consists in the possession of capacities of a certain kind for living the sort of life that is characteristic *of that kind*. The capacities that constitute life will be different for different kinds of creatures. 'Living' is predicated of different kinds of creatures neither univocally nor equivocally, but, rather, analogically. This is the character of the continuity of living among all living creatures. 'Living' is in this respect, like 'good' and 'healthy.'[16] The cessation of life, death, will be different but analogous for different kinds of creatures.

Were someone to point to a heap of quivering corpses at the foot of the guillotine, and ask, "Are any of those living?,," Madame Defarge might sensibly respond, "Are any of those living *what?*" The point of this response is that there are in that heap many living cells, some living tissues, but no living human beings.

---

16. For further discussion of these matters, see my *Virtues and Vices*, pp. 25–32.

I am not denying that there are important features that all living things share. All living creatures, perhaps, are composed of one or more living cells. The presence of living cells, however, is not in general sufficient for the presence of a living creature of some other kind. The fact, then, that life is found in creatures who lack a certain capacity is not an objection to defining death in *other* kinds of creatures as the loss of that capacity.

Our being alive, accordingly, is a matter of our having capacities for doing and experiencing. These capacities may be impaired to a considerable extent, and we still have a human life, although it is a defective one. In some extreme cases of mental retardation, advanced senility, insanity, and so on, it may be unclear whether *any* capacity for human life remains. Given the value of human life, and the hard fact that once a life is ended it cannot be recovered, it is reasonable in such conditions of uncertainty to insist that such severely incapacitated individuals be regarded as living human beings. When an individual is comatose and it is not known whether the coma is irreversible, then such an individual is alive. Cases in which it is *known* with certainty that a coma is irreversible were encountered only relatively recently. The decision whether such individuals are alive or dead effectively changes our ideas of human life and death, and the case for deciding that such individuals are dead is strong. The case for this redefinition or revision of the idea of death is based upon facts about human life and concerns, and thus the redefinition it indicates can fairly be said to rest upon the real nature of life and death. When, therefore, there is good reason to extinguish the life in cells and tissues in the body of someone irreversibly comatose, we need not be deterred for fear of taking a human life. This is not an argument for euthanasia in the case of the irreversibly comatose. The point is that such individuals are already dead.

From the fact that a physician can reasonably regard a patient known to be irreversibly comatose as dead, it follows that the physician need not be concerned about killing the patient or preserving the patient's life. It does not follow, of course, that the physician should not be concerned about the feelings and beliefs of the friends and relatives of the deceased patient and take these into account in deciding how the patient's remains are to be treated. Even if we and the physician know the patient is dead, there remains a serious problem if a relative will not accept the fact. My purpose in this discussion is to make a case for accepting a certain redefinition of death. Problems will remain to be solved.

THE VIEW of the value of human life to which I have appealed is substantially the inheritance of the Judeo-Christian moral tradition; it is the view of the community in which I was raised. Some people claim that if we were consistent, we would value the life of certain other living creatures as much as human life and extend the requirements of protecting and preserving human life to these other creatures. I maintain that the lives of severely incapacitated human beings are entitled to the same protection as the lives of normal human beings as long as there is any possibility of the incapacitated individuals' participating in the doings and experiences that comprise a human life. Yet there are beasts that possess capacities for activities and experiences comparable to those of certain severely incapacitated human beings. Why are not the lives of these other animals valued equally with human lives? Since it is regarded as morally unobjectionable, with certain important qualifications, to kill beasts for food or in scientific research, it is claimed that our moral views about the value of life are inconsistent. Peter Singer writes:

> When we decide to treat one being — the severely and irreparably retarded infant — in one way, and the other being — the pig or monkey — in another way, there seems to be no difference

[156]

between the two that we can appeal to in defense of our discrimination. There is, of course, the fact that one being is, biologically, a member of our own species, while the others are members of other species. This difference, however, cannot justify different treatment, except perhaps in very special circumstances; for it is precisely the kind of arbitrary difference that the most crude and overt kind of racist tries to use to justify racial discrimination. Just as a person's race is in itself nearly always irrelevant to the question of how that person should be treated, so a being's species is in itself nearly always irrelevant.[17]

The claim that treating an incapacitated human being in one way and a monkey or a pig in another, in the way that we do, is morally arbitrary cannot be sustained, however. A monkey or a pig does not present us with the sorts of problems we face with an incapacitated man or woman or a defective infant. These unfortunate human beings stand in a variety of important relationships to the rest of us that are different from the relations to us of pigs and monkeys. The former are members of families and communities, while the latter are not. If one thinks of an "irreparably retarded human infant" as *merely* an organism with such and such capacities and a pig as merely an organism with the same capacities, then one will see no difference between them. Consider, however, the fact that the infant is someone's child, and consider the many difficult and painful problems created for a family and for a community by a defective infant or a severely incapacitated adult. We have good reason to devise ways of dealing with these problems in the form in which they confront us — that is, as problems for people who live in families and communities, with all the complex ways, habits, and feelings that are a part of such living. What-

17. Peter Singer, "Unsanctifying Human Life," in John Ladd, ed., *Ethical Issues Relating to Life and Death* (New York: Oxford University Press, 1979), p. 47.

ever ways we devise for dealing with such problems must be as compatible as possible with our other ways. It would be folly to ignore these matters. It is not at all surprising that our ways of dealing with defective infants and incapacitated adults, developed as they are as part of a complex social context, are not automatically extended to our dealings with pigs and monkeys, nor is this arbitrary. Recognition of these points does not require us to abandon a critical attitude toward existing morality, nor does it force us to condone cruelty to animals.

There is a tendency to dismiss an argument such as this on the grounds that it is simply an appeal to "conventional morality." It is true that the argument appeals to existing social arrangements, including moral practices, and it is also true that social arrangements are conventional in some sense (perhaps in more than one sense). The sense in which morality is conventional, however, is not incompatible with there being good reasons for existing moral practices and beliefs — reasons we ignore at our peril. It is tempting to respond that what is really arbitrary is to declare that for moral purposes, *all* that matters about human beings is that they are organisms with certain capacities, ignoring the complex and important relations of the beings to one another and to the social context in which they live. One consequence of doing this is that familiar distinctions of great importance are made to appear groundless and inexplicable.

Suppose I were to set a genuine silver dollar next to a clever counterfeit of one and insist that these are *merely* pieces of metal with such properties as shape, weight, and chemical composition. After adopting this view of the two coins, I might be unable to find any differences between them that would account for the importance that people attach to the fact that one is genuine and the other counterfeit. My problem, however, is not to be explained by the hypothesis that our having different attitudes toward genuine and counterfeit coins (coins with different histories) is arbitrary. The view I have taken up divorces the coins from their crucial connections with money, commerce, and government — their roles in our lives and activities. It severs these coins from their internal relations with the social context that makes them what they are. Generally, things are what they are and have the properties they have because of their relationships to other things. This is true of matters having to do with values and standards of correctness. A perspective or view that tears such things from their contexts, severing these relations, will so distort matters that familiar and intelligible things will appear strange and inexplicable.

THE ENTERPRISE of redefining death, then, need not be viewed as an ad hoc adjustment in conventional meaning that is meant to hide the fact that something morally objectionable is being done to comatose individuals. The project of redefinition is not optional. The permanent cessation of heartbeat and respiration was the *sine qua non* of human death as long as we had no other reliable indicator of the permanent cessation of the capacity for doing and experiencing. At least one other reliable indicator of irreversible coma has been discovered. Apparently, with minor qualifications, an individual who shows all the criteria of "brain death" (according to the criteria proposed by the Ad Hoc Committee of the Harvard Medical School to Examine the Definition of Brain Death) is irreversibly comatose. Death should be redefined in such a way that individuals who are "brain-dead" are dead, even though their "vital signs" continue. There are individuals who are in a "persistent vegetative state" but who retain brain-stem function and breathe spontaneously. Such people — Karen Quinlin was the most publicized case — are not "brain-dead." If there are in such cases reliable indicators that the coma is irreversible — that the capacity for doing and experiencing is completely and irrecoverably lost — then such indicators should be adopted as criteria of death too. In view of the value of human life and the importance of

[159]

protecting the most helpless of us, the definition of death should be drawn in such a way that where it is not known with reasonable certainty that an individual's coma is profound and irreversible, the individual is not dead but alive. Where it is known by means of reliable indicators that an individual is irreversibly comatose, then — in the most reasonable interpretation of the words 'living human being' in formulations of the moral requirements that we protect and preserve human life — that individual is not a living human being. The requirements are not relevant in such cases.

BIBLIOGRAPHY

Anscombe, G. E. M. "Modern Moral Philosophy." *Philosophy* 33 (1958), 1-19.

Aristotle. *The Politics of Aristotle*. Ed. and trans. Ernest Barker. Oxford: Clarendon Press, 1946.

Aristotle. *The Works of Aristotle Translated into English*. Ed. Sir W. David Ross. 12 vols. Oxford: Oxford University Press, 1915.

Brandt, Richard B. *A Theory of the Good and the Right*. Oxford: Clarendon Press, 1979.

"A Definition of Irreversible Coma: Report of the Ad Hoc Committee of the Harvard Medical School to Examine the Definition of Brain Death." *Journal of the American Medical Association* 205 (1968), 337-340.

Dewey, John. *Art as Experience*. New York: Putnam, 1934.

Dewey, John. *Human Nature and Conduct*. New York: Henry Holt, 1922.

Donagan, Alan. "Is There a Credible Form of Utilitarianism?" In Michael D. Bayles, ed., *Contemporary Utilitarianism*. Garden City, N. Y.: Doubleday, 1968.

Finnis, John. *Natural Law and Natural Rights*. Oxford: Clarendon Press, 1980.

Foot, Philippa, *Virtues and Vices*. Berkeley: University of California Press, 1978.

[161]

Green, Michael B. and Daniel Wikler. "Brain Death and Personal Identity." *Philosophy and Public Affairs* 9 (1980), 105–114.

Hampshire, Stuart. *Two Theories of Morality*. Oxford: Oxford University Press, 1977.

Hare, R. M. *The Language of Morals*. Oxford: Clarendon Press, 1952.

Hsu, Immanuel C. Y. *The Rise of Modern China*. New York: Oxford University Press, 1970.

Kant, Immanuel. "On a Supposed Right to Tell Lies from Benevolent Motives." In *Kant's Critique of Practical Reason and Other Works on the Theory of Ethics*, ed. and trans. Thomas K. Abbott. London: Longmans, Green, 1909.

King, Martin Luther, Jr. "Letter from Birmingham City Jail." In Hugo Adam Bedau, ed., *Civil Disobedience: Theory and Practice*. New York: Pegasus, 1969.

McCloskey, H. J. "A Non-Utilitarian Approach to Punishment." In Michael D. Bayles, ed., *Contemporary Utilitarianism*. Garden City, N.Y.: Doubleday, 1968.

MacIntyre, Alasdair. *After Virtue*, 2d ed. Notre Dame: University of Notre Dame Press, 1984.

McNeill, William. *The Rise of the West*. Chicago: University of Chicago Press, 1963.

Marcus, Ruth B. "Moral Dilemmas and Moral Consistency." *Journal of Philosophy* 77 (1980), 121–136.

Moore, G. E. *Ethics*. London: Oxford University Press, 1912.

Murphy, Arthur E. *The Theory of Practical Reason*. La Salle, Ill.: Open Court, 1967.

Parfit, Derek. *Reasons and Persons*. Oxford: Clarendon Press, 1984.

Patterson, Orlando. *Slavery and Social Death*. Cambridge: Harvard University Press, 1982.

President's Commission for the Study of Ethical Problems in Medicine and Biomedical and Behavioral Research. *Defining Death: Medical, Legal, and Ethical Issues in the Determination of Death*. Washington, D.C.: U.S. Government Printing Office, 1981.

Putnam, Hilary. *Reason, Truth, and History*. Cambridge: Cambridge University Press, 1981.

Quine, W. V. "Review of Milton K. Munitz, ed., *Identity and Individuation*." *Journal of Philosophy* 69 (1972), 490.

Raphael, D. D. "The Standard of Morals." *Proceedings of the Aristotelian Society* 75 (1974-75), 1-12.

Rawls, John. *A Theory of Justice*. Cambridge: Harvard University Press, 1971.

Rawls, John. "Two Concepts of Rules." *Philosophical Review* 64 (1955), 3-32.

Ross, W. D. *Foundations of Ethics*. Oxford: Clarendon Press, 1939.

Ross, W. D. *The Right and the Good*. Oxford: Clarendon Press, 1930.

Scheffler, Samuel. *The Rejection of Consequentialism*. Oxford: Clarendon Press, 1982.

Schneewind, J. B. "Moral Knowledge and Moral Principles." *Knowledge and Necessity*, Royal Institute of Philosophy Lectures 3 (1968-69), 249-262.

Schneewind, J. B. *Sidgwick's Ethics and Victorian Moral Philosophy*. Oxford: Clarendon Press, 1977.

Sidgwick, Henry. *The Methods of Ethics*. 7th ed. London: Macmillan, 1907.

Singer, Peter. "Unsanctifying Human Life." In John Ladd, ed., *Ethical Issues Relating to Life and Death*. New York: Oxford University Press, 1979.

Smart, J. J. C., and Bernard Williams. *Utilitarianism: For and Against*. Cambridge: Cambridge University Press, 1973.

Taylor, Charles. "The Diversity of Goods." In Amartya Sen and Bernard Williams, eds., *Utilitarianism and Beyond*. Cambridge: Cambridge University Press, 1982.

Thoreau, Henry D. "Civil Disobedience." In Hugo Adam Bedau, ed., *Civil Disobedience: Theory and Practice*. New York: Pegasus, 1969.

Urmson, J. O. "Aristotle's Doctrine of the Mean." *American Philosophical Quarterly* 10 (1973), 223-230.

Urmson, J. O. "A Defense of Intuitionism." *Proceedings of the Aristotelian Society* 75 (1974-75), 111-119.

Wallace, James D. *Virtues and Vices*. Ithaca: Cornell University Press, 1978.

Walzer, Michael. *Spheres of Justice*. New York: Basic Books, 1983.

Warren, Mary Anne. "On the Moral and Legal Status of Abortion." *The Monist* 57 (1973), 43-61.

Will, Frederick L. *Induction and Justification*. Ithaca: Cornell University Press, 1974.

Will, Frederick L. "Pragmatic Rationality." *Philosophical Investigations* 8 (1985), 120–142.

Will, Frederick L. "The Rational Governance of Practice." *American Philosophical Quarterly* 18 (1981), 191–201.

Wittgenstein, Ludwig. *Philosophical Investigations*. Trans. G. E. M. Anscombe. New York: Macmillan, 1953.

INDEX

[165]

Index

Library of Congress Cataloging-in-Publication Data

Wallace, James D., 1937–
  Moral relevance and moral conflict.

  Bibliography: p.
  Includes index.
  1. Ethics. I. Title
BJ1012.W352   1988   170   87–47961
ISBN 0-8014-2096-2 (alk. paper)